QUESTIONS AND ANSWERS
ON PRACTICAL COOKERY

Victor Ceserani MBE, CPA, MBA, FHCIMA

Formerly Head of
The Ealing School of Hotelkeeping and Catering,
Polytechnic of West London

Ronald Kinton B.Ed (Hons), FHCIMA

Formerly of
Garnett College, College of Education
for Teachers in Further and Higher Education

David Foskett B.Ed (Hons) FHCIMA

Fellow of the Academy of Culinary Arts,
Director of Hospitality Education and Training at the
Polytechnic of West London

To accompany Practical Cookery *seventh edition*

Hodder & Stoughton
LONDON SYDNEY AUCKLAND

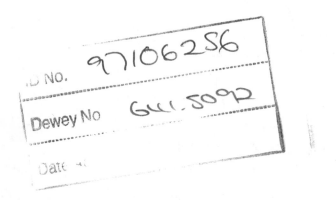
British Library Cataloguing in Publication Data

Kinton, Ronald
  Questions and answers on practical cookery.
  I. Title   II. Ceserani, Victor
  641.507

  ISBN 0-340-55639-0

First published 1976
Second edition 1981
Third edition 1987
Impression number 10 9 8 7 6 5 4 3 2
Year   1998   1997   1996   1995   1994   1993

Typeset by Wearside Tradespools, Boldon, Tyne and Wear
Printed in Great Britain for the educational publishing division of Hodder and Stoughton Ltd, Mill Road, Dunton Green, Sevenoaks, Kent by St Edmundsbury Press Ltd, Bury St Edmunds, Suffolk

CONTENTS

INTRODUCTION

The aim of this book is to assist catering students in their revision by providing questions drawn mainly from the seventh edition of *Practical Cookery* and their own general knowledge of the subject.

Questions are set out in chapters following the *Practical Cookery* format and each chapter commences with a number of short answer questions followed by questions in depth.

The answers are given, mainly in brief outline together with page references to the main text, and follow at the end of each chapter. Many of the answers use key words to assist students to develop a more coherent and comprehensive explanation. Where examples are requested, only specimen answers are given so as to encourage the student to think.

It is the authors' opinion that systematic revision throughout the training years related to the practice of cookery can assist in giving a deeper understanding and knowledge of the subject.

This book should be helpful to students taking catering courses in schools, NVQs Levels I, II, III, IV, City and Guilds of London examinations at all levels, BTEC certificate and diploma courses, membership of the Hotel, Catering and Institutional Management Association examinations, degree students as well as those who have an interest in the subject.

KNIVES, USEFUL INFORMATION AND HEALTHY EATING
(Chapters 1 and 2)

Short Questions . . . .

1 State 10 safety rules to be observed when using knives.

2 State three basic qualities which ensure enjoyment of food.

3 a. What is the approximate metric equivalent of:

1oz	½lb	¼pt	½in
4oz	¾lb	¾pt	2in
6oz	1½lb	1½pt	6in
10oz	2lb	2pt	1ft?

b. What is the Fahrenheit equivalent of the following oven temperatures? 130°C; 150°C; 200°C; 220°C; 250°C

4 Give the centigrade oven temperatures for these regulo numbers: 1; 3; 5; 7; 9

5 What important advisory committee on nutrition do the initials NACNE stand for?

6 What variations can affect the fat content of meat?

7 Place the following commodities in order showing the one with lowest % of saturated fat first: Beef dripping; Butter; Ground nut oil; Soft margarine; Sunflower seed oil; Olive oil

8 Fill in the blanks:

> Natural yoghurt in place of cream.
> . . . in place of animal fat.
> Instead of white flour use . . . Skimmed milk instead of . . . in place of full fat cheese.

9 What do you understand by the term pathogens?

10 When giving nutritional information how is the energy content expressed?

11 What is the nutritional effect of adding: a. prawns as a garnish to a soup   b. cream and egg yolks?

12 Suggest three uses for nutritional analysis of recipes.

Questions in depth . . . .

1 a. Explain the 8 safety rules to be considered when using knives.

b. Indicate the procedure for sharpening knives and the removal of stains, making particular reference to hygiene and safety.

2 a. When considering a healthy diet what are the chief ingredients that should be used in moderation?

b. Name the four medical conditions that can develop if we do not follow a healthy diet.

c. The National Advisory Committee on Nutrition recommends a maximum daily intake of energy (calorie) intake sufficient to maintain optimum body weight total fat, saturated fat, sugar, dietary fibre and salt. Give these figures in grams per day.

d. Discuss the caterers role in maintaining the nation's health.

3 a. Discuss six ways in which nutritional analysis can be used?

b. What does the following nutritional analysis for 1 portion breadcrumbed veal, ham and cheese escalope reveal? 627kcals–48.1g fat of which 16.3g is saturated; 12.0g carbohydrate of which 1.3g is sugars, 37.1g protein, 0.7g fibre

c. State the format for nutritional information.

d. What is the effect of: i. adding prawns to a fish soup and ii. enriching a sauce with cream and egg yolks?

Short Questions ● Answers . . . .

1 knife point down;   flat on table;   not over table edge;   keep eye and mind on job;   correct knife for specific purpose; sharpness;   wipe after each use;   handles clean;   not left in sink;   not mis-used

2   inviting;   appetising;   pleasant taste   *p23 PC*

3   a. 25g   200g   125ml   1cm
        100g   300g   375ml   5cm
        150g   600g   750ml   15cm
        250g   1Kg   1 litre   30cm

    b. 250°F;   300°F;   400°F;   425°F;   500°F

4   140°C;   160°C;   190°C;   220°C;   250°C

5   National Advisory Committee on Nutrition Education   *p24 PC*

6   breed;   how fed;   how butchered

7   sunflower seed;   olive;   ground nut;   soft margarine;   beef
    dripping;   butter

8   vegetable oil;   wholemeal flour;   full cream milk;   low fat
    cheese

9   harmful germs (disease-forming organisms)

10 kilocalories or kilojoules   *p28 PC*

11 a. increases protein content;   b. increases fat content   *p29 PC*

12 e.g. recipe handouts;   menu labelling schemes;   customer
    information   *p23 PC*

Questions in depth • Outline answers . . . .

1   a. sharpness;   use of correct knife;   carrying of knives;   table
        position;   concentration;   wiping correctly;   cleanliness;
        safety when washing;   misuse;   handles kept clean   *p12 PC*

    b. sharpening steel and carborundum stone, grinding angle,
        strength and procedure for using steel and stone. When using
        a stone always draw the blade of the knife away from the
        hand. When using a steel always keep the knife being
        sharpened away from you. Safety procedure, cleaning of

stains — use fine cleaning powder or abrasive
pad. *p14–17 PC*

2 a. fat; sugar; fibre; salt *p23 PC*

    b. obesity; heart disease; some cancers; some diseases of the
digestive system *p24 PC*

    c. fat 80–85g; sugar 50g; saturated fat 20/25g; dietary fibre
5g; salt 5g *p24 PC*

    d. Caterers skill, knowledge
In UK about one third meals eaten daily provided by caterers
Bad practice — overloading dishes with fat and sugar
Increasing consumer demand
Revise menus, production, service techniques
Marketing and promotion skills *p26 PC*

3 a. menu labelling e.g. traffic light scheme; recipe cards,
customer hand-outs; posters, leaflets; articles for media;
healthier standard recipes; specific marketing initiatives e.g.
healthy eating days *p32 PC*

    b. 1 portion provides — state per portion or per recipe;
express energy content as kilocalories or kilojoules; total
fat listed with saturated fat; need to aim for more starchy
carbohydrate and less sugar; protein content; fibre
content *p28 PC*

    c. a working man may need 2600–2900kcals daily; maximum
recommended amount of fat for average person 80–85g;
starch and sugar content of dish low; a working man may
need about 75g protein daily; negligible fibre
content *p30 PC*

    d. i. increase protein content; ii. increase fat content
particularly saturated fat *p29 PC*

METHODS OR PROCESSES OF COOKERY
(Chapter 3)

Short Questions . . . .

1 What is the effect of heat on food in the following:
   a. protein; b. vitamin D; c. vitamin C?

2 What is the effect of dry and moist heat on the carbohydrates
   starch and sugar?

3 State three important points to be observed if the maximum
   vitamin C is to be retained when cooking vegetables.

4 List 12 methods or processes of cooking food.

5 Give a definition for boiling.

6 Give examples of foods cooked by boiling using: a. fish;
   b. vegetables; c. meat

7 What particular consideration applies when boiling salted or
   pickled meats e.g. silverside of beef?

8 Approximately how long per ½kg (1lb) is allowed for boiling
   meat?

   15 minutes; 20 minutes; 25 minutes; or 30 minutes

9 Vegetables grown above the ground are cooked in: cold
   water; warm water; hot water; or boiling water

10 Vegetables such as turnips and cauliflower should be boiled
    gently otherwise they will: taste strong; lose colour; become
    mashed; or lose flavour

11 State three advantages of boiling.

12 Name four essential safety practices when boiling.

13 Define poaching.

14 Name three different foods with examples which may be cooked
    by poaching.

15 a. Specify two points which must apply when poaching food.

   b. To which food, when poached, do the general rules not apply?

16 Give the definition for stewing.

17 Why does the stewing of meat have nutritional advantages?

18 Which of the following meats is suitable for stewing?   coarser types;   tender cuts;   prime joints;   or young carcass

19 Name a dish of each of the following cooked by stewing:
a. meat;   b. poultry;   c. vegetables

20 State four safety points to be observed when stewing.

21 Give a definition for braising.

22 a. What are the two methods of braising?

   b. Give an example of a dish cooked by each.

23 What is meant by each of the following terms associated with braising: a. sealing;   b. marinating;   c. sweating;   d. browning?

24 Why is it necessary to use a pan with a tight fitting lid when braising: to protect the contents;   to prevent coloration;   to prevent evaporation;   or to increase coloration?

25 What is the ideal oven temperature for braising?

26 Meat may be marinaded before braising in a mixture of: wine, vegetables and herbs;   stock, vegetables and herbs;   vinegar, vegetables and spices;   or wine, herbs and spices

27 Name four vegetables which may be braised.

28 Briefly describe two different ways of steaming food.

29 Give the definition for steaming.

30 State 3 points of safety to be observed when steaming foods.

31 Name four foods suitable for cooking by steaming.

32 What is meant by cooking sous-vide?

33 State three advantages of sous-vide.

34 Name 2 foods suitable for cooking sous-vide.

35 Explain the difference between baking and roasting.

36 How does the heat of the oven cook a baked jacket potato?

37 Why are egg custards cooked in a bain-marie?

38 Toad in the hole is: a. sausage in batter;   b. sausage roll;
    c. a hot dog;   or d. a ham roll

39 Why is time and temperature control so essential when baking?

40 What is meant by 'recovery time' when using baking ovens?

41 State four general rules for baking.

42 Define oven roasting.

43 What is meant by basting meat: inserting pieces of fat meat;
    batting out with a cutlet bat;   spooning the cooking fat over the
    meat;   or covering with a slice of fat?

44 Why is basting necessary: to flavour the fat;   to prevent
    drying;   to colour gravy;   or to increase evaporation?

45 Beef when roasted should be well done: true/false?

46 Why is it essential to commence roasting in a pre-heated oven?

47 What is the difference between a conventional general purpose
    oven and a convection oven?

48 When roasting pork should you allow approximately: 25
    minutes per ½kg and 25 minutes over;   20 minutes per ½kg
    and 20 minutes over;   15 minutes per ½kg and 15 minutes
    over;   or 10 minutes per ½kg and 10 minutes over?

49 a. What are the approximate cooking times per ½kg (1lb) for roasting: Beef; Lamb?

b. Name two vegetables which may be roasted.

50 What is the purpose of a meat thermometer?

51 Why should joints of meat or poultry be roasted on a trivet or grid?

52 A fast method of cooking by radiated heat describes which method of cookery?

53 Which is the odd one out and why: cooking on a grill; cooking under a salamander;   cooking on a spit;   or cooking between grill bars?

54 Describe: a. three different ways of grilling food and;   b. give a menu example for each.

55 Why are grill bars pre-heated and brushed with oil before use?

56 What are the nutritional effects of grilling?

57 Name four terms, both English and French, which describe the degrees of grilling steaks.

58 a. Tomatoes and mushrooms are grilled under the . . . ?

b. Name four foods suitable for cooking on a griddle.

59 Why are certain foods grilled on trays?   to improve the flavour;   to prevent them falling between grill bars;   to cook them more slowly;   or to colour them more evenly

60 Define two methods of frying.

61 Explain the meaning of the terms *sauté* when applied to cooking poultry or meat.

62 What is meant by the term meunière and to what type of food is it usually applied?

63 Define stir-frying.

64   What are the effects of shallow-frying on food?

65   Give eight points essential to ensure safe deep frying.

66   Why is it necessary to coat most foods which are to be deep fried?

67   Name three coatings which may be used to coat foods for deep frying.

68   Which of the following fruits are suitable for coating in batter and deep frying: bananas; apples; pineapples; strawberries; cherries; oranges?

69   Why is it essential to strain deep fat after each use?

70   Explain the principle of microwave cookery.

71   Can a microwave oven be used for defrosting food?

72   What is standing time related to microwave cookery?

73   What two major disadvantages has microwave cookery?

74   Give three advantages of microwave cookery.

75   Why is a microwave oven so useful for reheating food?

76   Define pot-roasting.

77   Give three examples of food that may be pot-roasted.

78   When pot-roasting, what are the food juices and the bed of roots use for after the food is cooked.

79   a. Why is presentation so important in the appearance of cold food?

     b. Give three basic principles to achieve this.

80   Where should cold food be kept before, during and after assembling before final garnishing?

Questions in depth . . . .

1   a. List 12 methods or processes of cooking food.
        With the minimum of repetition suggest *two* different foods
        suitable for cooking by each method.

    b. Write each dish as it would appear on a menu.

Boiling

2   a. Define boiling as a method of cookery and name four liquids
        in which foods can be boiled.

    b. Give *two* menu examples of each of the following foods
        cooked by boiling. Fish, meat, poultry, vegetables.

    c. i. What are the advantages of boiling related to meats and
            poultry

       ii. what is the approximate cooking time per 400g (1lb) for
            boiling salted or pickled meat?

    d. Discuss the four safety points associated with boiling.

Poaching

3   a. Define poaching as a method of cookery and its purpose.

    b. What are the two methods of poaching food? Give two menu
        examples for each.

    c. What do the following techniques mean?   cutting and
        tying;   folding;   draining;   reducing for sauce

    d. Why are time and temperature important when poaching
        food?

Stewing

4   a. Define stewing and its purpose as a method of cookery.

    b. What are the various methods of stewing?

    c. What are the effects of stewing?

    d. Suggest two dishes from each of the following cooked by
        stewing: meat;   poultry;   vegetables

5   a. What are the advantages of stewing?

    b. What are the safety rules that should be observed?

c. What is the procedure for care and cleanliness of pans used for stewing?

d. Name four items of equipment that can be used for stewing.

Braising

6   a. Give the definition for braising and its purpose.

b. Describe the two methods of braising and give two different menu examples for each.

c. What are the effects and advantages of braising?

d. Explain the following techniques: sealing;   larding;   marinating;   sweating

Steaming

7   a. Define steaming and state its purpose.

b. Describe the various methods of steaming.

c. What are the effects and advantages of steaming?

d. Give two menu examples of food cooked by steaming from each of fish, meat, vegetables, sweets.

8   a. Discuss the method and advantages of vacuum cooking in a pouch known as sous-vide.

b. What are the essential safety precautions to be observed when using steamers?

c. What are the following techniques?   moulding;   traying-up;   loading;   preparation of container

Baking

9   a. State the definition and purpose of baking.

b. What are the methods and effects of baking?

c. What are the advantages of baking?

d. Describe the following techniques: marking;   brushing;   cooling;   finishing;   recovery time;   dusting

Roasting

10   a. Define roasting and explain the various methods.

b. What are the effects and advantages of roasting?

c. How are time and temperature controlled?

d. What are the safety points when roasting?

Grilling

11 a. Give the definition for grilling and explain the various methods and the effects.

b. Explain in detail the degrees of grilling meat, the equivalent French terms and describe the appearance of the juice issuing from the meat.

c. Give two menu examples for each of the following foods cooked by grilling — fish, meat, vegetable, savoury.

d. List the general rules for efficient grilling and the safety precautions that should be observed.

Shallow frying

12 a. State the definition and explain the methods of shallow frying.

b. Give the effects and advantages of shallow frying and two menu examples for each of the following foods:
eggs; fish; meat; poultry; vegetables; sweets

c. Suggest three items of small equipment and two items of large equipment suitable for shallow frying.

d. Give the safety rules essential for shallow frying.

Deep frying

13 a. Give definition and the methods of deep frying.

b. What are the effects and advantages?

c. Explain in detail the requirements for efficient and safe deep frying.

d. Give a menu description for ten deep fried foods.

Microwave

14 a. Define in detail the principles of the microwave as used in an oven and the various types of food that can be cooked.

b. List the advantages and disadvantages.

c. List the special points for attention when cooking and factors which affect efficient cooking.

d. What are the advantages of the microwave/convection oven?

Cold preparation

15 a. Correct hygiene practices regarding personal habits, food and equipment are essential at all times, particularly when dealing with cold food. Summarise these hygiene practices.

   b. Discuss the preparation for cold work.

   c. What should be the characteristics of cold food?

   d. Suggest six appetising cold buffet dishes.

Short Questions • Answers ....

1   a. coagulates; b. not destroyed; c. easily lost (water soluble)   *p37 PC*

2   starch — dry heat causes colour changes
         moist heat causes grains to soften and swell
  sugar — dry heat causes caramelisation
         moist heat dissolves   *p37 PC*

3   do not soak in water;   cook in small quantities;   cook quickly and do not overcook;   cut at the last minute   *p39 PC*

4   boiling; poaching; stewing; braising; steaming; baking; roasting; grilling; deep and shallow frying; paperbag; microwave; pot-roasting

5   cooking in liquid at boiling point (100°C)   *p38 PC*

6   e.g. a. turbot; salmon; cod
        b. cabbage; carrots; swedes
        c. silverside of beef; bacon; leg of mutton

7   may require soaking depending on the salt content   *p279 PC*

8   30 minutes to the pound plus 30 minutes

9   boiling water

10 become mashed

11 e.g. older, tougher, cheaper meat and poultry made palatable and digestible; nutritious stock results; labour saving *p41 PC*

12 correct size of container; move pans carefully; position of handles; care when handling boiling liquid *p41 PC*

13 cooking in minimum liquid just below boiling point *p42 PC*

14 e.g. eggs—poached eggs on spinach with cheese sauce
      fish—poached Finnan haddock
      fruit—assorted fruit compote

15 a. temperature control; strict control of cooking time

    b. eggs *p41 PC*

16 slow cooking of food cut in pieces, cooked in minimum liquid *p44 PC*

17 slow cooking converts meat connective tissue into gelatinous substance so that fibres fall apart and become digestible protein coagulated but not toughened; collagen forms into gelatine *p45 PC*

18 coarser types

19 a. Irish stew; b. chicken fricassée; c. ratatouille

20 e.g. suitable sized pans; care when removing hot pans from oven and when removing pan lids; sprinkle of flour on hot pans when off stove *p47 PC*

21 cooking in liquid or sauce in covered pan in oven. *p47 PC*

22 a. brown; white *p48 PC*

    b. beef olives; braised celery

23 a. application of heat to meat surface to prevent escape of juices; b. steeping in richly spiced liquid for flavour; c. extraction of flavour without coloration; d. colouring a surface by application of heat *p49 PC*

24 to prevent evaporation

25 160°C (gas mark 3)

26 wine, vegetables, herbs

27 e.g. onions, leeks, endive, celery

28 e.g. atmospheric or low pressure;   high pressure in purpose
        built equipment   *p50 PC*

29 cooking under various degrees of steam pressure (moist heat) at
     or above atmospheric pressure   *p50 PC*

30 e.g. allow steam pressure to reduce before opening door;   take
        care not to scald oneself when opening door;   check water
        level and ball valve arms where applicable   *p53 PC*

31 e.g. potatoes, vegetables, fish, sponge puddings

32 food contained in vacuum-sealed plastic pouches cooked by
     steam   *p51 PC*

33 e.g. minimal change of texture and weight loss;   food cooks in
        own natural juices;   uniformity of standard   *p51 PC*

34 e.g. cuts of fish;   breast of chicken   *p51 PC*

35 baking cooks by dry oven heat;   roasting cooks by moist oven
     heat

36 steam builds up from the water content in the potato and
     combines with dry heat to cook it   *p54 PC*

37 to modify the heat, cook more slowly and lessen the risk of
     overcooking the egg mixture

38 a. sausage in batter

39 unless ovens are heated to the correct temperature before goods
     are inserted they will be spoiled

40 time required for ovens to reach the correct temperature before cooking a further batch of food

41 e.g. accuracy in weighing and measuring; temperature control; utilise oven space efficiently; correct preparation of trays and moulds   *p56 PC*

42 cooking in dry heat with oil or fat in an oven or on a spit *p57 PC*

43 spooning the cooking fat over the meat

44 to prevent drying

45 false, it should be cooked medium

46 to seal the surface protein and prevent escape of natural juices   *p57 PC*

47 air circulation — in a conventional oven the temperature varies in different parts of the oven. In a convection oven the powered fan gives an even temperature all over

48 25 mins per lb plus 25 mins

49 a. Beef 15 minutes; Lamb 20 minutes

    b. e.g. potatoes; parsnips

50 to determine the exact temperature in the centre of the meat being roasted

51 to raise the joint from the fat in the roasting tray and prevent it frying

52 grilling

53 on a spit — this is roasting; the other three are methods of grilling

54 a. over heat; under heat; between heat   *p60 PC*

    b. e.g. a grilled steak; mushrooms; toasted sandwich

55 to prevent food sticking

56 because of the speed of cooking there is maximum retention of nutrients and flavour

57 rare — au bleu; under done — saignant; just done — á point; well done — bien cuit

58 a. Salamander

   b. hamburgers; sausages; eggs; pancakes

59 to prevent them falling between grill bars

60 shallow — cooking food in a small quantity of pre-heated oil or fat; deep — cooking in pre-heated deep oil or fat   *p67 PC*

61 small pieces of poultry or meat rapidly cooked on both sides in a sauté or frying pan   *p64 PC*

62 meunière is the cooking of floured fish in shallow fat or oil on both sides and finishing with lemon juice, nut-brown butter and chopped parsley   *p64 PC*

63 fast frying of small pieces of food in a little oil in a wok or frying pan

64 the high temperature produces almost instant coagulation of surface protein of the food thus retaining natural juices   *p65 PC*

65 e.g. do not over-fill deep fat fryer; dry food thoroughly; do not overload deep fat fryer; place food in carefully   *p70 PC*

66 protect food surface from excess heat; prevent escape of moisture and nutrients; modify penetration of intense heat   *p68 PC*

67 milk and flour; egg and crumbs; batter

68 bananas; apples; pineapple

69   food particles remaining in fat will brown and spoil fresh food
     being fried   *p70 PC*

70   high frequency power from a magnetron develops microwaves
     at a high frequency which activate water molecules or particles
     of food and agitates them causing heat by friction   *p71 PC*

71   yes

72   removing certain foods e.g. scrambled eggs while underdone as
     they will complete cooking in standing time   *p72 PC*

73   not suitable for all foods, limited oven space   *p72 PC*

74   e.g. time saving, speed, economical on energy

75   because the food is heated quickly   *p71 PC*

76   cooking on bed of root vegetables in a covered pan   *p74 PC*

77   chicken;   fillet of beef;   pheasant

78   the basis of a sauce to coat or accompany the food

79   a.   should stimulate the appetite

     b.   clean and fresh appearance;   eye appealing presentation;
          not over decorated or handled   *p76 PC*

80   in a cool place, cold room or refrigerator.   *p77 PC*

Questions in depth ● Outline answers ....

1 a. Methods	Suitable foods	b. Menu examples
boiling	beef silverside	boiled silverside of beef, dumplings, onions, carrots
poaching	eggs	poached eggs with cheese sauce *oeufs pochés mornay*
stewing	lamb	lamb stew with vegetables *navarin printanier*
braising	duck	braised duck and peas *canard braisé aux petits pois*
steaming	potatoes	new jersey potatoes
baking	apples	baked apple dumpling *pomme en cage*
roasting	pheasant	roast pheasant *faison rôté*
grilling	mushrooms	mushrooms on toast
shallow frying	trout	shallow fried trout with almonds *truite meunière aux amandes*
deep frying	cod fillet	fried fillet of cod in batter *filet de cabilland à l'Orly*
paper bag	veal chop	*côte de veau en papillote*
microwave	smoked haddock	smoked haddock *haddock fumée*
pot-roasting	chicken	pot-roasted chicken with mushrooms *poulet poêlé aux champignons*

2   a. cooking of prepared foods in liquid at boiling point
water, milk, stock, court-bouillon   *p38 PC*

     b. e.g. boiled turbot hollandaise sauce
boiled silverside, dumplings and carrots
cream of chicken soup
Vichy carrots

     c. i. old, tough, cheap cuts are rendered palatable,
fuel economy,   suitable large scale cookery,
nutritious;   labour saving

       ii. cooking time 20 minutes per lb plus 20 minutes over

     d. correct size containers;   movement of pans on stove;
position of pan handles;   adding or removing foods from
containers of boiling liquids   *p41 PC*

3   a. cooking of foods in liquid below boiling point
easy to digest, tender texture, makes food safe to eat and
pleasant to taste   *p42 PC*

     b. shallow e.g. Filets de sole Dugléré
deep e.g. poached eggs on spinach with cheese sauce

     c. cutting food in even pieces tying to retain shape;   making
neater and smaller;   drying off cooking liquor from food
before coating with sauce;   straining off cooking liquor and
reducing quantity by rapid boiling   *p43 PC*

     d. control of temperature to ensure cooking liquor does not fall
below correct degree;   control of time ensures food properly
cooked   *p43 PC*

4   a. slow cooking of food in pieces in minimum liquid on top of
stove or in oven;   makes cheaper cuts suitable, economic,
nutritional   *p44 PC*

     b. combination of unpassed ingredients;   thickening cooking
liquor;   cooking in the sauce on the stove or in the oven
covered with a lid   *p44 PC*

     c. during slow process connective tissue converted to gelatine;
protein coagulated but not toughened;   lower cooking
temperature   *p45 PC*

     d. e.g. Irish stew;   chicken curry;   ratatouille

5   a. meat juices retained; little evaporation; nutrients conserved; tenderises; economical   *p45 PC*

     b. suitable size pans; care; removal of lids; warning on hot pans; pan handles   *p47 PC*

     c. wash hot detergent water; rinse hot water; dry; grease moving parts; corret pan storage; check loose handles; tin linings on copper pans   *p46 PC*

     d. saucepans; boiling pans; bratt pans; ovenproof dishes

6   a. cooking in liquid in covered pan in the oven gives variety, tenderises, and makes food digestible, palatable   *p47 PC*

     b. brown — sealed, browned, flavourings added, oven cooked e.g. beef olives
white — blanched, refreshed, cooked in white stock e.g. braised celery

     c. breakdown of tissue fibre, softens texture, tenderises, less expensive meats can be used, retention of nutrients, variety on menu   *p48 PC*

     d. applying heat to meat surface; inserting fat in strips; steeping in pickling liquid; extracting flavour   *p49 PC*

7   a. cooking of prepared foods by moist heat; to make food digestible, of edible texture, safe, nutritious   *p50 PC*

     b. low pressure; high pressure; between plates over a pan of boiling water   *p50 PC*

     c. change in structure and texture; retention of nutrients, digestible, speed, labour-saving
batch cooking, economical   *p51/2 PC*

     d. e.g. steamed halibut, shrimp sauce; steak and kidney pudding; pommes vapeur (steamed potatoes); orange sponge pudding

8   a. food cooked in vacuum sealed plastic pouches by steam; minimal changes in texture/reduced weight loss, labour saving; no drying out/colour loss; food cooks in own juices   *p51 PC*

b. check water levels if applicable;   ball arm moves freely; reduce steam pressure before opening door to reduce risk of scalds   *p53 PC*

c. placing of food in prepared moulds;   filling of steamer trays with moulds;   placing trays in steamer;   moulds clean and lightly greased   *p52 PC*

9 a. cooking of food by dry heat in an oven;   make food digestible, palatable, safe;   eye appeal;   variety of textures; popularity   *p53 PC*

b. dry baking plus steam from food;   increased humidity/ addition of water or steam in oven;   bain-marie/heat modification   *p54 PC*

c. variety;   eye appeal;   aromas;   uniformity of bulk cooking;   ovens with effective temperature controls;   easy access for loading/removal   *p55 PC*

d. cutting with sharp blade;   egg, sugar or milk brushed on before or after cooking;   use of wire grids/air circulation; presentation improvements;   time required for oven temperature to return to correct degree before continuing cooking;   light sprinkling of flour, or icing or castor sugar

10 a. cooking in dry heat with fat in oven or on spit to cook food tender, digestible, safe, palatable   *p57 PC*

b. surface protein of meat sealed to help retain natural juices succulent — juices for gravy;   controlled energy use and temperature;   minimal fire risk   *p58 PC*

c. ovens pre-heated;   oven temperatures in recipes followed; cooking time affected by shape, size, type, bone formation and quality meat thermometers

d. suitable sized trays;   careful handling;   suitable dry cloths; food securely held before removal from tray   *p60 PC*

11 a. quick cooking by radiant heat;   over heat — on preheated greased bars;   under heat — salamander;   between heat — between grill bars or plates;   speed of cooking — maximum retention of nutrients   *p60/1 PC*

b. rare — au bleu — red and bloody

underdone — saignant — reddish pink
just done — à point — pink
well done — bien cuit — clear   *p61* **PC**

c. e.g. grilled herring — mustard sauce; mixed grill; grilled
     tomatoes; Welsh rarebit

d. seal and colour on hot grill; basting — use of tongs, palette
   knives; care when moving hot salamander and grill bars;
   use edged trays; care when removing foods   *p63* **PC**

12 a. cooking food in small quantity of fat in shallow pan or flat
      surface;
      shallow fry — meunière — presentation side first
      sauté — tender meat in sauté or frying pan — deglazing
      griddle — solid metal plate   *p64* **PC**
      stir fry — fast cooking in wok or frying pan   *p65* **PC**

b. instant coagulation of protein retaining juices; change in
   nutritional content; quick rapid cooking   *p65* **PC**

Menu examples

shallow fried eggs with bacon
oeufs frits au lard

shallow fried plaice fillets with
cucumber
*filets de plie meunière aux
concombres (Doria)*

shallow fried sirloin steak with red
wine sauce
entrecôte sauté bordelaise

breadcrumbed breast of chicken
with asparagus
suprême de volaille princesse

shallow fried Belgian endive
endive Belge meunière

shallow fried banana flamed with
rum
banane flambé au rhum

c. e.g. omelette pan;   bratt pan   *p66 PC*

d. correct pan size;   sleeves rolled down;   care when placing
   food in hot fat;   thick, clean dry clothes for cleaning;   move
   loaded hot pans carefully on stove   *p67 PC*

13 a. cooking of food in deep fat or oil;   coat with milk and flour
       — batter — egg and crumb etc.;   blanching — partial deep
       frying   *p67/8 PC*

    b. surface sealed, minimum absorption of fat on coated items;
       uncoated items absorb more fat;   partial cooking or
       blanching helps busy service;   wide variety of foods
       possible;   coated food quickly sealed;   fast cooking;   easy
       handling   *p68 PC*

    c. systematic working;   no overfilling;   never allow fat to
       overheat;   no excess of food in fryer;   allow recovery time;
       reduce temperatures as business slackens — restrict holding
       time;   strain fat daily;   cover fat when not in use;   half fill
       fryers;   no overloading;   dry food;   place food in fat
       carefully;   basket and spider to hand;   fire equipment;
       sleeves down;   thick, dry, clean cloths for handling   *p70 PC*

    d. e.g. Scotch eggs and salad;   fish cakes, tomato sauce;
       croquette potatoes;   French fried onions;   doughnuts

14 a. high frequency power;   electricity agitation of water
       molecules in food causing heat/friction;   cooks raw food;
       re-heats cooked food;   defrosts frozen food   *p71 PC*

    b. time saving;   fast;   economical on energy and labour;
       meals available 24 hours a day;   food cooks in own juices;
       minimal shrinkage and drying-out flexibility;   not suitable
       for all foods;   limited cooking space;   penetration depth of
       microwaves limited   *p72 PC*

    c. correct selection of cooking/time controls;   certain foods
       e.g. fish — remove when underdone to finish cooking;   use
       suitable containers e.g. glass, china etc;   cook even-shaped
       items;   keep food level/not mounds;   sufficient space for
       storing;   cover most foods   *p73 PC*

    d. speed, coloration, use of metal pans   *p73 PC*

15 a. danger to food — chemical e.g. copper
                          plant e.g. toadstools
                          micro-organisms e.g. bacteria

    food poisoning sources;   spreading methods;   growth
    factors;   potentially dangerous foods e.g. made-up meat
    dishes;   preventions — care of person;   of food;   of
    environment   *p76 PC*
                                        (*p369/70 T of C*)

    b. adequate mise-en-place;   work flow;   food kept cool;
        garnish and decorate close to service time   *p77 PC*

    c. appearance clean and fresh, eye appealing, appetite
        stimulating, nutritional value   *p76 PC*

    d. e.g. dressed crab;   chicken and ham pie;   orange bavarois

CULINARY TERMS
(Chapter 4)

Short Questions . . . .

1   What do you understand by the term offal?

2   What are giblets: poultry offal; fish fillets; type of bacteria; or a rice dish?

3   What is French for 'in the style of' as used in menus?

4   'À la carte' and 'carte du jour' are two common terms; explain 'à la carte'.

5   What are bacteria: micro-organisms; harmful rays; small insects; or minute animals?

6   Give three explanations of the term 'bain-marie'.

7   What are bean sprouts?

8   Which is used during roasting: a. breading; b. blanc; c. basting; or d. ballottine

9   'Blanching' is a common culinary term with five meanings; define blanching in five ways.

10   What are crudités?

11   How do bouchées and vol-au-vents differ?

12   Match the following:

a. brunoise	thin strips
b. paysanne	½cm (¼″) dice
c. macédoine	small dice
d. julienne	thin rounds, triangles or squares

13   A canapé is a dish cover: true/false.

14   Carbohydrates consist of 3 groups; name all three.

15 What is the value of calcium to the diet? Does it: prevent skin disease; build bones and teeth; provide vitamin C; or give energy?

16 What is the culinary meaning of clarification?

17 *Clostridium perfringens* are food poisoning bacteria; where are they found?

18 What is understood by 'correcting' when related to a soup or a sauce?

19 Explain the difference between a darne and a tronçon.

20 Deglaze means to serve on ice: true/false.

21 What is duxelle: chopped mushrooms and onions — cooked; chopped mushrooms and shallots — cooked; chopped mushrooms and breadcrumbs — cooked; or chopped mushrooms and minced meat — cooked?

22 Give two examples of emulsions used in the kitchen.

23 How are the two emulsions in your answer to question 22 used?

24 When are petits fours served?

25 Explain the difference between a blanquette and a fricassée.

26 Garam masala — what is it?

27 A liaison is for: tiering; turning; thickening; trussing

28 Give three different examples of the use of the term 'to glaze'.

29 What is the difference between mirepoix and macédoine?

30 Monosodium glutamate is used to increase flavour: true/false.

31 If the term 'Native' is on the menu what would it signify:

a dish for locals; okra fingers; English oysters; or a speciality?

32 What is the French term for food which has been egg and crumbed: piqué; beignet; bardé; or pané?

33 What is a pulse: a dried pod vegetable; a savoury rice; a vegetable soup; or a dried fruit?

34 The term 'refresh' is frequently used in cookery; what does it mean?

35 If working in the pastry what could you prove?

36 What is *salmonella* and where is it found?

37 What is *staphylococcus* and where is it found?

38 What is the culinary meaning of 'to sweat'?

Short Questions ● Answers . . . .

1 inner organs of animals e.g. heart, liver, etc.

2 poultry offal

3 à la

4 dishes prepared to order and priced individually

5 micro-organisms

6 e.g. containers of water   *p80 PC*

7 young shoots of dried beans

8 basting

9 make white; retain colour; remove skin; make limp; cook without colour   *p81 PC*

10 pieces of raw vegetables served as an appetiser   *p82 PC*

11 bouchées are smaller in size

12 a. small dice

    b. thin, neat shapes

    c. ¼″ dice

    d. thin strips

13 false, it is a cushion of bread for hot or cold foods   *p81 PC*

14 sugar; starch; cellulose

15 builds bones and teeth

16 to make clear, as in consommé, jelly

17 in the soil, vegetables and meat

18 adjusting; seasoning; consistency; colour

19 darne — slice of round fish on bone, e.g. salmon
    tronçon — slice of flat fish on bone, e.g. turbot

20 false, it means to swill out a pan in which food has been
    cooked   *p82 PC*

21 chopped mushrooms and shallots, cooked

22 mayonnaise; hollandaise

23 salad dressing etc; warm sauce served with various foods e.g.
    fish

24 with coffee after a meal

25 blanquette — the meat is cooked in stock from which a white
    sauce is made   *p259 PC*
    fricassée — the food is cooked in the white sauce   *p364 PC*

26 a ready prepared mixture of spices

27 thickening e.g. a velouté soup

28 to colour; to finish pastries; to finish vegetables   *p83 PC*

29   mirepoix — roughly cut vegetables;   macedoiné — neatly cut cubed vegetables or a mixture e.g. fruit salad

30   true

31   English oysters

32   pané

33   dried pod vegetable

34   make cold under running water

35   yeast dough

36   food poisoning bacterium found in meat and poultry

37   food poisoning bacterium found in the human throat and nose, also in septic cuts

38   to cook in fat under a lid without colour

STOCKS AND SAUCES
(Chapter 5)

Short Questions . . . .

1   Explain what is understood by the term 'stock' when it relates to a liquid used in the kitchen.

2   Why is beef stock cooked for a longer time than fish stock?

3   Stock goes cloudy if it is: boiled insufficiently;   boiled for too long;   boiled too slowly;   or boiled too quickly

4   State four points which indicate a good stock.

5   To achieve good quality stock it is necessary to:

6   Salt is omitted from stock because: it prevents it from simmering;   it causes it to go sour;   it makes it change colour; or stock is used as a base for many dishes

7   Why is it necessary to skim stock?

8   What is the purpose of having brown and white beef stock in the kitchen?

9   What are the proportions of ingredients needed for stock (other than fish stock)?

10   Describe the difference between producing a brown stock and a white stock.

11   Why is the time taken to cook fish stock important?

12   What are fish glaze and meat glaze?

13   Fish glaze and meat glaze are used to: increase flavour;   save money and time;   improve the appearance;   or improve texture

14   A sauce is a thickened liquid; name four ways in which the liquid can be thickened.

15   State four points which indicate a good quality sauce.

16 A roux is: a thickening; a type of saucepan; an unusual vegetable; or a Russian sweet

17 Name 3 roux and 3 stocks and give an example of a suitable sauce for each.

18 Why should a boiling liquid never be added to a hot roux?

19 Name three ingredients which may be used to thicken jus lié.

20 What is understood by the word 'dilute': to add liquid; to drain in a colander; to pass through a sieve; or to put in a bain-marie?

21 How many portions will four litres of white onion sauce produce?

22 What two main items are needed to produce a velouté?

23 Name four velouté sauces.

24 What two items may be used to finish a velouté sauce?

25 Caper sauce is served with: boiled mutton; boiled bacon; boiled beef; or boiled fish

26 A sauce . . . is used in chicken vol-au-vent.

27 Name three sauces which are derivatives of sauce suprême.

28 Which of the following is produced from espagnole sauce: caper sauce; ivory sauce; demi-glace sauce; or béarnaise sauce?

29 Name 6 sauces which are derived from a refined brown sauce.

30 What is the name of the sauce which contains chopped shallots, sliced mushrooms, tomatoes, chopped parsley and tarragon?

31 Sauce diable may be served with: grilled meat; cold meat; roast meat; or boiled meat

32 What is the main ingredient in sauce lyonnaise: mushrooms; shallots; gherkins; or onions?

33 With what dish may sauce lyonnaise be served?

34 Chopped capers and chopped gherkins are used in: sauce Robert; sauce poivrade; sauce piquante; or sauce charcutière

35 Côtelette d'agneau Réforme is a well-known dish; describe sauce Réforme.

36 Which of the following sauces contains duxelle: piquante; Robert; italienne; or charcutière?

37 What points indicate a high standard of roast gravy?

38 Name two dishes with which bread sauce is served.

39 Why is apple sauce served with roast pork, duck and goose?

40 Cranberry sauce is served with roast turkey: true/false.

41 Match the following sauces with an appropriate dish.

a. bread	fried lamb cutlets
b. mint	roast chicken
c. tomato	fried liver
d. lyonnaise	roast lamb
e. curry	fried fish
f. Réforme	hard boiled eggs

42 Explain how the following are used: a. beurre fondu; b. beurre manié, and; c. beurre maître d'hôtel.

43 Name two different dishes with which hollandaise sauce may be served.

44 Why may hollandaise sauce curdle?

45 How can the curdling of hollandaise sauce be avoided?

46   How can curdled hollandaise sauce be rectified?

　　　by adding butter;   by whisking in a little hot water;
　　　by increasing the temperature;   by more whisking

47   What is the difference between hollandaise and béarnaise
　　　sauces?

48   When handling warm egg-based sauces what two factors can
　　　assist in the prevention of *salmonella* infection.

49   Why is a compound butter sauce served with grilled fish?

50   Give four reasons why mayonnaise may curdle.

51   Name two sauces which are thickened by using eggs.

52   Sauce verte could be served with

　　　cold turbot;   cold beef;   cold ham;   cold salmon

53   Which ingredients are needed to produce tartar sauce from
　　　mayonnaise sauce?

54   With what dish is horseradish sauce served?

　　　roast beef;   roast lamb;   roast veal;   roast venison

55   Mint sauce is traditionally served with

56   Why is it very important to observe hygienic standards when
　　　using aspic jelly and chaudfroid sauce?

57   What points of quality would indicate a high standard aspic
　　　jelly?

58   Sauces such as tomato, béchamel etc. form a skin on the surface;
　　　suggest how this can be prevented.

Questions in depth . . . .

1   a. Give the principles for making good stock.

　　　b. What are the differences between making white meat, brown
　　　　 meat, fish, and vegetable stocks?

c. Describe a glaze, the method of making and its use.

d. Give the definition of a sauce, four ways in which a sauce can be thickened and two menu examples from each method.

2 a. What is a roux, what are the three degrees to which it may be cooked, what safety precaution should be observed when adding liquid to a roux?

b. Name three fats or oils that can be used for making a roux.

c. What is meant by dextrinisation and what can be its effect in a roux?

d. Name the basic sauce and two derivations that can be made from: white; blond; brown roux.

3 a. Give the proportion of ingredients and method of making: i. roast gravy; ii. jus lié; iii. bread sauce; iv. apple sauce; and suggest a suitable dish with which each could be served.

b. Give method of making; horseradish; mint; and, Cumberland sauces

and suggest a suitable dish with which each could be served.

c. Name three compound butter sauces, give the ingredients for each and a suitable dish with which each could be served.

4 a. Explain the method of making hollandaise sauce and state the proportion of ingredients required.

b. Give reasons why it may curdle and the remedy

c. What essential points regarding food safety and hygiene must be observed when making and keeping the sauce warm?

d. Give three menu examples of the use of this sauce and describe and name a related sauce with a menu example.

Short Questions ● Answers . . . .

1 a liquid containing some of the soluble nutrients and flavours of food which are extracted by gentle simmering   *p90 PC*

2 because 20 minutes is sufficient to extract the flavour from fish bones whereas 6–8 hours are required for beef bones

3   boiled too quickly

4   flavour; colour; clarity; non-greasy

5   use sound ingredients; bring to the boil, skim then simmer; skim frequently; do not over or under cook

6   stock is used as a base for many dishes and if the stock were salted, as it reduced in cooking the end product could be over-salted

7   to remove grease and scum and retain the quality of the stock

8   white stock for white stews, sauces, soups etc; brown stock for brown stews, sauces, soups etc.

9   bones 4lbs; water 1 gallon; vegetables 1lb   *p91 PC*

10 for a brown stock the bones and vegetables are coloured. For white stock bones and vegetables are used raw

11 overcooking spoils flavour

12 fish and meat stock steadily reduced to a sticky consistency   *p92 PC*

13 increase flavour

14 roux; egg yolks; cornflour etc.; beurre manié   *p92 PC*

15 smooth; glossy appearance; definite taste; light texture

16 a thickening

17 white roux — milk — Béchamel; blond roux — stock — velouté; brown roux — stock — demi-glace

18 because heavy steam will result which could cause a burn or scald

19 cornflour; arrowroot; potato flour

20 to add liquid

21 60–80 portions

22 blond roux;   stock

23 caper;   suprême;   mushroom;   ivory

24 egg yolks and cream

25 boiled mutton

26 suprême

27 aurore;   ivory;   mushroom

28 demi glace

29 Bordelaise;   chasseur;   devil;   poivrade;   Italian;   Madeira

30 chasseur

31 grilled meat

32 onions

33 e.g. Vienna steaks

34 sauce piquante

35 a well flavoured demi-glace or jus lié with the addition of
red-currant jelly and a garnish of julienne of beetroot, egg white,
gherkin, mushroom, truffle, tongue   *p103 PC*

36 Italienne

37 appetising brown colour;   not greasy;   good flavour

38 roast chicken;   roast pheasant

39 because the sharpness of the apple sauce complements the
richness of the flesh and aids digestion

40 true

41 a. roast chicken

b. roast lamb

c. fried fish

d. fried liver

e. hard boiled eggs

f. fried lamb cutlets

42 a. as an accompaniment to asparagus, sea-kale, salmon etc.   *p107 PC*

b. equal quantities of butter or margarine and flour kneaded to a smooth paste mixed into boiling liquid.   *p94 PC*

c. all the ingredients are mixed, shaped into a roll, wrapped in wet greaseproof paper or foil, refrigerated then cut into thick slices just before serving   *p109 PC*

43 e.g. poached salmon;   trout;   broccoli

44 Sabayon incorrectly made;   too fierce heat;   butter added too quickly   *p108 PC*

45 whisk egg yolks over gentle heat, allow to cool slightly, add butter slowly.   *p108 PC*

46 by whisking onto a little hot water

47 the reduction, consistency and final addition to béarnaise   *p109 PC*

48 use pasteurised egg yolks;   discard after keeping warm for 2 hours

49 because if thick slices are placed on the fish just prior to the fish being served, it will just begin to melt and be soft for the customer to use

50 oil added quickly;   oil too cold;   insufficient whisking;   stale egg yolks   *p111 PC*

51 mayonnaise;   béarnaise

52 cold salmon

53 gherkins; capers; parsley

54 roast beef

55 roast lamb

56 because they both contain gelatine, a meat based product*, and
    are likely to become contaminated if not kept and used under
    refrigeration *a suitable medium for bacterial growth

57 crystal clarity; appetising colour; good flavour

58 add a thin layer of butter on top of the sauces

Questions in depth ● Outline answers . . . .

1 a. foundation of many preparations; maximum care
       necessary; use sound ingredients; remove scum;
       degrease; simmer; maintain temperature; no salt;
       refrigerate if kept   *p90 PC*

   b. white stock — bones blanched
       brown stock — bones and vegetables browned   *p90/1 PC*
       fish stock — 20 minutes cooking only   *p212 PC*
       vegetable stock — 1 hour cooking only   *p381 PC*

   c. reduced stock; reduce stock to gelatinous consistency;
       used for flavour strengthening or improving   *p92 PC*

   d. lightly thickened liquid; roux, beurre manié,
       arrowroot, egg yolks; e.g. béchamel, moules marinières,
       jus lié, hollandaise

2 a. combination fat and flour
       white; blond; brown
       never add boiling liquid to hot roux   *p93 PC*

   b. butter; margarine; vegetable oil; dripping

   c. chemical change in flour; sauce may become thin because
       the starch is broken down and loses its thickening
       property   *p93 PC*

    d. béchamel e.g. mornay sauce;   velouté e.g. suprême sauce; espagnole e.g. chasseur sauce

3   a. i.   roast gravy for roast meats e.g. roast leg of lamb — 1pt stock, 8oz bones, 5oz vegetables all browned and simmered for 2 hours   *p104 PC*

           ii. jus lié for pot roasted meat or chicken — well flavoured brown stock or roast gravy lightly thickened with diluted arrowroot or cornflour   *p105 PC*

          iii. bread sauce with roast game, roast chicken — ¾pt milk flavoured with studded onion, thickened with breadcrumbs   *p106 PC*

          iv. apple sauce with roast pork — 1lb apples, 1oz sugar, 1oz butter cooked to puree   *p106 PC*

          i.   roast beef; ii. roast veal; iii. roast chicken; iv. roast pork

    b. combine grated horseradish, vinegar, cream — roast beef; combine chopped mint, vinegar, sugar — roast lamb; combine redcurrant jelly, chopped shallots, port, lemon, orange, mustard — cold ham   *p112/3 PC*

    c. parsley — 12oz butter, parsley, lemon juice — grilled steak anchovy — butter and anchovy essence — grilled sole shrimp — 2oz butter, 2oz shrimps — grilled plaice   *p109 PC*

4   a. reduction (optional) yolks cooked and sabayon, melted butter whisked in — 2 yolks, 8oz butter   *p108 PC*

    b. excess heat — butter added too quickly use a teaspoon of boiling water and/or another yolk and slowly whisk on the curdled mixture

    c. pan, whisk and strainer perfectly clean, butter fresh sauce kept in clean receptable for service use pasteurised yolks, do not keep sauce warm longer than two hours, then discard

    d. boiled turbot, asparagus, cauliflower béarnaise — grilled steak

HORS-D'OEUVRE, SALADS AND SANDWICHES
(Chapter 6)

Short Questions . . . .

1   What do you understand by the term 'hors-d'oeuvre'?

2   Into what two main categories may hors-d'oeuvre be divided?

3   What accompaniments are served with oysters?

   brown bread and butter and lemon;   white bread and butter
   and lemon;   melba toast and lemon;   toast and lemon

4   From which fish is caviar obtained: shad;   salmon trout;
   sturgeon;   or salmon?

5   What part of the fish is caviar: the roe;   the marrow;   the
   young fish;   or the brain?

6   How should smoked salmon be carved?

7   How should oysters be served: in a coupe;   on a canapé;   on a
   julienne of lettuce;   or on crushed ice?

8   How many oysters are usually served as a portion: four;
   five;   six;   or eight?

9   Pâté is usually cooked in a: timbale;   sauteuse;   terrine;   or
   ravier

10   For grapefruit cocktail the grapefruit is cut into: halves;
   quarters;   segments;   or dice

11   State the points which indicate a well prepared grapefruit
   cocktail.

12   What have the following in common; ogen, charentais,
   honeydew and cantaloup?

13   Name four juices which can be served as a first course.

14   Suggest three ways of serving avocado pear.

15   The basic sauce for a shellfish cocktail is: mayonnaise; béchamel;   hollandaise;   or fish velouté

16   When buying crabs what points of quality should be considered?

17   When purchasing crabs why is it wise to buy them alive?

18   What sauce is usually served with dressed crab: sauce verte; sauce mayonnaise;   sauce tartare;   or sauce hollandaise?

19   What part is discarded when preparing dressed crab: gills; claws;   antennae;   legs?

20   What is the culinary meaning of 'soused':   pickled in alcohol; kippered in smoke;   cooked in vinegar;   saturated in oil?

21   Name two kinds of fish which may be soused.

22   Suggest two ways of presenting a variety of hors-d'oeuvre.

23   Egg mayonnaise is presented in three ways on the menu; describe each, stating how much egg per portion would be used.

24   Suggest six points to be considered when preparing a selection of hors-d'oeuvre.

25   Compile a list of eight items that can be included in a selection of hors-d'oeuvre.

26   Name five items which could be prepared à la grecque.

27   If a dish is termed à la portugaise which ingredient will be included: tunny;   cucumber;   sweetcorn;   or tomato?

28   Name eight food items which could be served at a cocktail party.

29   What does the word canapé indicate: specific garnish; Russian cake;   cushion for food;   or sliced sausage?

30   Suggest six bouchée fillings.

31   What is the difference between a simple salad and a composed salad?

32   A dressing should always be offered with any salad: true/false.

33   Name four suitable ingredients that may be added to vinaigrette in order to give variation.

34   What is added to cream in order to make an acidulated cream dressing?

35   What are the four chief ingredients added to vinaigrette to make Thousand Island dressing?

36   What ingredients could you serve in a bowl of mixed salad?

37   What are the usual ingredients in a French salad?

38   A Florida salad consists of: lettuce and grapes;   lettuce and grapefruit;   lettuce and orange;   or lettuce and tomato

39   What dressing would you offer with a Florida salad?

40   Give the ingredients of a Japanese salad.

41   The chief ingredients of a Salad Niçoise are:

French beans, anchovies, potatoes, capers, olives, tomatoes
French beans, peas, carrots, turnips, anchovies, olives
French beans, tomatoes, potatoes, anchovies, olives, turnips
French beans, lettuce, onions, pimentos, anchovies, olives

42   Suggest four different types of bread suitable for sandwiches.

43   Suggest an interesting variety of six sandwich fillings.

44   Suggest four examples of combination fillings for sandwiches.

45   Suggest five different seasonings that are suitable for varying the flavour of sandwiches.

46   Which of the following would you sprinkle on to a dish of sandwiches? chopped parsley; watercress; mustard and cress; or shredded lettuce .

47   What is a toasted sandwich?

48   Give two examples of popular toasted sandwiches.

49   Two slices of hot buttered toast with a filling of lettuce, grilled bacon, sliced hard boiled egg, slice of chicken and mayonnaise is known as:

savoury toasted sandwich; book-maker sandwich; jumbo sandwich; club sandwich

50   What is the name given to an underdone minute steak between two slices of hot buttered toast?

51   What are the following? double decker sandwich; treble decker sandwich

52   Give two examples for each: double decker; treble decker

53   Give a brief description of an open sandwich.

54   Suggest four interesting varieties of open sandwich.

55   Open sandwiches are traditionally prepared with: fresh bread; or toast

56   List six hygiene factors which must be taken into account when preparing sandwiches.

57   List four materials that can be used for packing sandwiches.

Questions in depth . . . .

1   a. Name the three categories into which hors-d'oeuvre can be divided. Give an example for each and describe the ingredients and method for preparing each item.

b. Give ingredients and method for a basic vinaigrette and suggest further ingredients that can be used for variation.

    c. Give the balance of ingredients and method of making mayonnaise, suggest two derivations and name two menu items for each.

    d. Give the reasons why a mayonnaise may turn or curdle and how it can be re-thickened.

2   a. Name and give ingredients for two compound salads from a vegetable base and two from a fruit base.

    b. Give ingredients and method for making a liver pâté.

    c. State three ways by which cross contamination between cooked and uncooked food can be prevented.

    d. How are avocado pears tested for ripeness, name and give ingredients for three ways of serving avocado pears and describe how the avocado is peeled, sliced and fanned.

3   a. Briefly describe eight interesting varieties of hors-d'oeuvre

    b. List ingredients and method of preparing coleslaw and celeriac salad

    c. Give ingredients and method for hors-d'oeuvre à la grecque and indicate four items that can be prepared by this method.

    d. i. What ingredients would be served for a green salad and

      ii. a mixed salad?

      iii. What dressing can be offered?

4   a. What are cocktail or reception canapés and what size should they be? Suggest six cold and six hot items.

    b. Suggest six different fillings suitable for savoury bouchees.

    c. Name six types of bread from which sandwiches can be made. Give examples of fillings for; three single items and three combinations. What seasonings can be added to flavour sandwich fillings?

    d. What is the approximate difference in the number of kcals between one round of sandwiches made with wholemeal bread and polyunsaturated margarine and white bread and butter?

Short Questions ● Answers . . . .

1   appetising first course dishes

2   single food items;   selection of dishes

3   brown bread and butter and lemon

4   sturgeon

5   the roe

6   in thin slices on the slant   *p120 PC*

7   on crushed ice

8   six

9   terrine

10 segments

11 neatly cut segments, no pips, no white pith

12 all types of melon

13 e.g. pineapple, orange, grapefruit, tomato

14 e.g. with vinaigrette, crabmeat, prawns

15 mayonnaise

16 they have both large claws, are heavy in comparison to size

17 to ensure that they are fresh

18 mayonnaise

19 gills

20 cooked in vinegar

21 herring;   mackerel

22 ready served on a plate — in raviers

23 a. as part of a selection of hors-d'oeuvre
        eggs quartered, halved or sliced lightly coated with
        mayonnaise

    b. an individual hors-d'oeuvre one egg   *p130 PC*

    c. as a main course two eggs

24 variety of choice, colour, ingredients, seasonings etc.

25 e.g. egg mayonnaise, salami, sardine, vegetable salad, meat
    salad, fish salad, tomato, rice salad

26 cauliflower, artichokes, button onions, leeks, celery

27 tomato

28 chicken bouchées, assorted canapés, game chips, celery sticks
    spread with cheese, etc.   *p143 PC*

29 cushion for food

30 e.g. mushroom, prawn   *p343 PC*

31 simple salad — individual item e.g. lettuce or tomato
    composed salad — combination of ingredients

32 true

33 e.g. English or French mustard, chopped herbs   *p119 PC*

34 lemon juice

35 pimento, egg, parsley, tomato ketchup   *p119 PC*

36 lettuce, tomato, watercress etc.   *p141 PC*

37 lettuce, tomato, cucumber

38 lettuce and grapefruit

39 sour cream

40   tomato, pineapple, orange, apple etc   *p138 PC*

41   French beans, anchovies, potatoes, capers, olives, tomatoes

42   white;   wholemeal;   rye;   caraway seed

43   ham, beef, egg, tuna fish, tomato, cucumber etc.

44   e.g. fish and lettuce, cheese and tomato   *p144 PC*

45   e.g. mayonnaise, mustard, chutney   *p145 PC*

46   mustard and cress

47   savoury filling between two slices of hot freshly buttered
      toast   *p145 PC*

48   e.g. ham, bacon

49   club sandwich

50   bookmaker sandwich

51   toasted and untoasted bread using three or four slices of bread
      with different fillings in between each layer

52   e.g. ham and tomato;   crispy bacon, lettuce, tomato

53   a buttered slice of bread generously covered with either meat,
      fish, egg, vegetable etc.

54   e.g. smoked salmon, lettuce;   potted shrimps, slice of lemon;
      shredded lettuce, slice hard boiled egg, cucumber,
      mayonnaise   *p146 PC*

55   fresh bread

56   clean protective clothing, hair covered, no nail varnish or finger
      jewellery, hands and finger-nails scrubbed clean, disposable
      gloves.

          clean utensils and work surfaces
          bread, spreads and fillings fresh, kept refrigerated before and

after making up. If to be kept, store in cool place
avoid cross-contamination e.g. fish, meat, eggs
all handlers to be trained in basic food and personal hygiene
ultra-violet fly killer

57 clingwrap, greaseproof paper, polystyrene containers,
polypropylene

Questions in depth ● Outline answers ....

1 a. i. Single cold food item e.g. smoked salmon, pâté,
grapefruit
e.g. 'halve the grapefruit, cut between segments serve
with a maraschino cherry in centre in a coupe   *p122 PC*

ii. a selection of cold dishes e.g. potato, meat, fish salads,
tomato, beetroot, sardine etc.
e.g. cooked sliced potatoes, chopped chive vinaigrette
bound with mayonnaise   *p132 PC*

iii. hot dishes e.g. champignons, bouchées
champignons à la portugaise — chopped onion, oil
tomatoes, garlic seasoning, mushrooms cooked together
and served hot   *p140 PC*

b. 3–6 parts oil to 1 part vinegar, mustard, salt, pepper
English/continental mustard, herbs, chopped egg, lemon
juice   *p119 PC*

c. ½pt oil, 2 yolks, seasoning, 2tspns vinegar
whisk yolks, vinegar, seasoning. Slowly mix in oil
finish boiling water
fried plaice fillets, tartar sauce — cold salmon trout, green
sauce   *p110 PC*

d. oil added quickly; oil too cold; insufficient whisking;
stale yolks; boiling water in clean bowl, slowly whisk in
curdled sauce or fresh yolk; with little water — whisk in
curdled sauce   *p110 PC*

2 a. e.g. Russian salad — carrots, turnips, peas, beans,
vinaigrette, mayonnaise   *p132 PC*
Waldorf salad — apple, celery, walnuts, mayonnaise,
lettuce   *p137 PC*

b. liver, fat, onion, garlic, herbs, pork, bacon
   liver, onion, garlic, herbs quickly fried, cooled, minced with
   pork in terrine (bacon-lined) cooked in bain-marie   *p121 PC*

c. use separate chopping boards for different foods e.g. meat,
   fish;   wash hands between handling raw and cooked foods;
   separate storage for raw and cooked food

d. base should give under gentle thumb pressure
   e.g. with shrimps bound with mayonnaise
            with crabmeat bound with shellfish cocktail sauce

   cut in half lengthwise, remove stone, peel off skin, slice
   lengthwise on to serving dish and fan-out   *p123 PC*

3   a. e.g. hard boiled eggs, mayonnaise
       potato salad — sliced cooked potatoes, chives, vinaigrette,
       mayonnaise
       meat salad — cooked meat, gherkins, French beans,
       tomatoes, vinaigrette, sliced tomato and cucumber
       three bean salad — three pulses, herbs, chives, vinaigrette
       fish salad — cooked fish, hard boiled egg, herbs, lettuce
       vinaigrette

    b. finely shredded cabbage, carrot, natural yoghurt or
       mayonnaise; fine julienne celeriac, lemon, mustard,
       mayonnaise, or yoghurt

    c. oil, lemon juice, herbs cooked with named vegetable
       e.g. artichokes, button onions, cauliflower, celery   *p139 PC*

    d. e.g. i.   lettuce (assorted)   *p115 PC* (illustration)

             ii.   lettuce, tomato, cucumber, watercress

             iii. vinaigrette in both cases   *p141 PC*

4   a. small food items — hot or cold served prior to main meals
       size — a comfortable mouthful
       cold — e.g. smoked salmon, sliced hard boiled egg on brown
       bread etc.
       hot — e.g. shrimp bouchées, mini-pizzas etc.   *p142 PC*

    b. e.g. mushrooms with chopped herbs in cream sauce
       diced vegetables in fromage frais   *p143 PC*

    c. white, wholemeal, rye, granary etc.

ham, cheese, sardine etc.
tuna fish and cucumber,
cheese, apple and chutney etc.
mayonnaise, mustard, chutney etc.   *p144 PC*

d. wholemeal kcals 237;   white kcals 338

polyunsaturated margarine 9·9g;   butter 19·4g

SOUPS
(Chapter 7)

Short Questions . . . .

1   Classify the soups.

2   Give an example for each class of soup.

3   How much soup is usually served per portion?   125ml (5fl oz); 250ml (10fl oz);   375ml (15fl oz);   or 500ml (20fl oz)

4   Suggest two ways of making a cream soup.

5   Specify the points which indicate a high standard consommé.

6   State the factors which are needed to produce a good quality consommé.

7   The colour of consommé should be: brown; amber; pale amber;   or dark brown

8   Suggest six garnishes suitable for adding to consommé and state how each should be written on the menu.

9   What have consommé en tasse and consommé madrilène in common?

10 Which stock is used to produce Scotch broth?   mutton;   beef; fish;   or chicken

11 Name the cereal used to garnish Scotch broth.

12 What characteristics has a broth of good quality?

13 A soup thickened by its main ingredient is called: velouté; purée;   broth;   or potage

14 Which class of soup is accompanied by croûtons?

15 Describe the points which indicate good quality croûtons.

16 The main ingredient for Crème St Germain is:

17 The main ingredient of a purée soissonnaise is: lentils; yellow split peas; haricot beans; or green split peas

18 The main ingredient of a purée parmentier is: potato; peas; potato and peas; or lentils

19 The garnish for purée cressonnière is: rice; carrot; watercress; or chicken

20 How is a good standard achieved when making a purée soup?

21 Name the two soups used to produce a Crème Solférino: potato and leek; potato and tomato; tomato and leek; potato and mushroom

22 What are the two French names for chicken soup?

23 Describe the flavour of mulligatawny soup:

24 Which garnish is served with mulligatawny soup?
   croûtons; rice; chicken; royale

25 Briefly explain the preparation of brown onion soup.

26 Describe how brown onion soup is served.

27 A flute is: diced fried bread; a roll; long thin loaf; or a cheese straw

28 What have kidney soup, thick mock turtle soup and thick oxtail soup in common?

29 Name the soup which is garnished with prunes, chicken and leek: cock-a-leekie; potage paysanne; minestroni; or mulligatawny

30 Minestroni originates from: Spain; Portugal; France; or Italy

31 What are the accompaniments to minestroni?

32 What does the term bisque indicate?

Questions in depth ....

1   a. Classify the different types of soup and give two examples
       for each

    b. Specify the ingredients and method of making consommé

    c. Explain the cause of the clarification process and give six
       reasons why consommé can go cloudy

    d. Give ingredients and method for making a royale

2   a. What is Vichyssoise and how is it prepared and served?

    b. What is Créme Solférino and how is it prepared?

    c. Give ingredients and method for Soupe à l'oignon

    d. What are: i. Mulligatawny;   ii. Cock-a-leekie;
       iii. Bisque?

Short Questions ● Answers ....

1   clear broth;   purée;   velouté;   cream;   bisque;
    miscellaneous   *p150 PC*

2   e.g. clear consommé;   Scotch broth   *p150 PC*

3   250ml 10fl oz

4   a purée finished with cream or/and milk
    a purée using half stock half béchamel   *p164 PC*

5   crystal clear;   no grease or fat;   good flavour

6   good fresh ingredients;   good quality stock;   careful method of
    clarification;   care when straining   *p152 PC*

7   amber

8   e.g. Consommé Royale;   Consommé brunoise   *p152 PC*

9   they are both served chilled

10 mutton

11 barley

12 well flavoured stock and plenty of vegetables

13 purée

14 purée

15 neatly and evenly cut, golden brown colour, crisp and good flavour

16 peas

17 haricot beans

18 potato

19 watercress

20 sound fresh ingredients, careful preparation and cooking, not overcooking, light consistency, good seasoning

21 tomato and potato

22 Créme de volaille;   Créme reine

23 gentle curry flavour

24 rice

25 finely sliced onions well coloured in butter, dusted with flour, good stock added

26 soup is poured into a suitable bowl, liberally sprinkled with sliced croûtons and grated parmesan cheese and gratinated   *p167 PC*

27 long thin loaf

28 all thick brown soups

29 cock-a-leekie

30 Italy

31 grated parmesan cheese; thinly sliced toasted flutes

32 shellfish soups

Questions in depth ● Outline answers . . . .

1 a. cream, purée, broth, consommé, bisque, velouté —
       miscellaneous
       cream of mushroom, purée Parmentier, Scotch broth,
       consommé royale, lobster bisque, velouté de volaille,
       minestroni   *p150 PC*

   b. beef, vegetables, egg whites, stock, seasoning
       mix minced beef, vegetables, egg whites, stock, bring slowly
       to boil. Simmer 2hrs, strain   *p151 PC*

   c. coagulation of egg albumen and meat absorbing all other
       ingredients as it rises to the top of the liquid
       e.g. greasy, poor quality stock, imperfect coagulation of the
       clearing agent   *p152 PC*

   d. egg, stock or milk, seasoning; whisked egg, liquid and
       seasoning cooked au bain-marie in dariole moulds

2 a. chilled creamed leek and potato soup with chives   *p159 PC*

   b. half cream of tomato and half potato soup, garnished carrots
       and potatoes   *p161 PC*

   c. onions, butter, flour, stock, bread, cheese
       browned sliced onions cooked in butter, stock added
       served with gratin top of bread and cheese   *p167 PC*

   d. i. curry soup; ii. chicken and veal stock garnished
          chicken, leek, prunes; iii. creamed shellfish
          soup   *pp168/169/173 PC*

EGGS AND FARINACEOUS DISHES
(Chapters 8 and 9)

Short Questions . . . .

Eggs

1 Describe what happens if scrambled eggs are overcooked.

2 When cooking scrambled eggs what points need particular attention?

3 When cooking scrambled eggs in bulk what precaution can be taken to reduce the risk of *salmonella* infection.

4 How long does it take to cook egg in cocotte?   1–2 minutes; 2–3 minutes;   3–4 minutes;   4–5 minutes

5 Suggest three suitable garnishes for egg in cocotte.

6 Match the appropriate cooking method of eggs to the approximate cooking time.

hard-boiled eggs	3–5 minutes
soft-boiled eggs	8–10 minutes
boiled egg	5½ minutes

7 Suggest four ways of using hard-boiled eggs.

8 Explain how Scotch eggs may be served: hot;   cold

9 At which meal is a boiled egg normally served?   breakfast; lunch;   dinner;   or supper

10 Describe a properly cooked poached egg.

11 Why is a little vinegar added to water when poaching eggs?

12 Match the following garnish with the appropriate dish

poached egg florentine	sweetcorn
poached egg Bombay	spinach
poached egg à la reine	curry
poached egg Washington	chicken

13 Why is it essential to use fresh eggs for poaching?

14   List five points which must be observed to produce a good omelette.

15   Name three flat omelettes. How are a Spanish omelette and an omelette fermiére served?

16   What is the garnish for each of the omelettes named in the previous question?

17   How does the finished appearance of a jam omelette differ from a savoury one?

18   What is the price of eggs?

Farinaceous dishes

19   What are farinaceous dishes?

20   What is the common term for the majority of farinaceous dishes?

21   Pasta dishes can be offered for any meal or snack: true/false.

22   Why is it necessary to cook spaghetti in plenty of boiling salted water?

23   Which of the following is usually served separately with farinaceous dishes?   croûtons;   sippets;   cheese;   rice

24   What points need particular attention when cooking pasta?

25   Give the names of four farinaceous dishes.

26   Which of the following is best served with farinaceous dishes?
     Cheddar;   Parmesan;   Gruyère;   Roquefort

27   What is the sauce used for spaghetti napolitaine?

28   List three items used to garnish spaghetti milanaise.

29   What shape is the garnish milanaise?   brunoise;   jardinière; paysanne;   or julienne

30   What is the main ingredient for bolognaise sauce?

     cheese;   tomatoes;   minced beef;   mushrooms

31   What is the French word for noodles?

32   Into what shape are noodles cut?

33   Puff paste is used to produce ravioli: true/false.

34   Explain the difference between canneloni and ravioli.

35   Name four dishes using pasta as a garnish.

36   Gnocchi means: pasta;   gnome;   bun;   or dumpling

37   Name three types of gnocchi and state the main ingredient of
each.

38   Why is it necessary to simmer gnocchi gently?

39   What is the difference between riz pilaf and risotto?

40   List four points which need particular attention when cooking
riz pilaf so as to achieve a good result.

41   Why is long-grained rice used for riz pilaf ?

42   Name two rice dishes which are included in the farinaceous
course of the menu.

43   Which of the following is not a farinaceous dish?   ravioli;
canneloni;   spaghetti italienne;   or brindisi au beurre

44   Match the appropriate sauce with the correct dish:

     béchamel   spaghetti bolognaise
     tomato   macaroni cheese
     demi-glace   spaghetti napolitaine

45   List six different types of manufactured pasta.

Questions in depth . . . .

Eggs

1   a. When using beaten eggs in large quantities e.g. omelettes, scrambled eggs, what procedure can be used to reduce risk of salmonella poisoning?

    b. What causes dark rings forming around yolks of hard boiled eggs?

2   a. Suggest six different methods of cooking eggs, give two menu examples for each method and state the food value of eggs.

    b. Explain the making of scrambled eggs and explain the effects of over-cooking.

    c. Outline the method for producing poached eggs.

    d. State the method for making omelettes, describe the three basic types and give a menu example for each.

Farinaceous

3   a. What is the difference between: i. ravioli; ii. canneloni; iii. lasagne?

    Describe a typical filling for canneloni.

    b. Which is the most suitable rice for a pilaff? Name and describe two dishes using pilaff. What is the difference between a pilaff and risotto?

Short Questions ● Answers . . . .

Eggs

1   protein toughens;   eggs discolour;   syneresis (water separation) occurs   *p178 PC*

2   slow cooking, constant stirring, remove from heat before cooking is completed   *p178 PC*

3   use pasteurised eggs

4   2–3 minutes

5   e.g. creamed minced chicken, tomato concassée   *p180 PC*

6   hard boiled eggs 8–10 minutes;   soft boiled eggs 5½ minutes;
    boiled egg 3–5 minutes

7   e.g. eggs chimay;   eggs aurore   *p181 PC*

8   hot with tomato sauce;   cold with salad   *p186 PC*

9   breakfast

10 firm tender white, slightly thickened unbroken yolk   *p183 PC*

11 to assist in setting the egg white and prevent it spreading

12 Florentine — spinach;   Bombay — curry;   Washington
    —sweetcorn;   à la reine — chicken

13 the white of stale or poor quality eggs will spread too thinly

14 e.g. clean hot pan, good fresh fat, lightly seasoned well beaten
    eggs, rapid cooking, not overcooking

15 e.g. Spanish;   Fermière   *p190 PC*

16 Spanish — tomato, onion, pimento;   Fermière — ham and
    parsley

17 jam omelette is sprinkled with sugar and caramelised

18 current market price

Farinaceous dishes

19 dishes containing flour or with a high starch content

20 pasta

21 false — any meal or snack time with the exception of breakfast

22 to prevent the strands from sticking together

23 cheese

24 plenty of boiling salted water, stir to the boil etc.   *p193 PC*

25 e.g. spaghetti with tomato sauce; macaroni cheese
   etc.   *p194–202 PC*

26 Parmesan

27 tomato

28 ham; tongue; mushroom

29 julienne

30 minced beef

31 nouilles

32 narrow strips

33 false, a noodle type paste is used

34 canneloni — filled tubes
   ravioli — savoury mixture sealed in paste   *p197–8 PC*

35 e.g. braised beef with noodles
        veal goulash
        veal escalope napolitaine
        poached chicken and rice

36 dumpling

37 parisienne — choux paste; romaine — semolina; piemontaise
   — potato

38 otherwise they will break up

39 pilaff (dry) cooked in oven, risotto (moist) on top of stove

40 e.g. correct type of rice, careful measurement, controlled
   cooking time, remove from cooking pan immediately   *p201 PC*

41 because it has a firm structure and retains its shape

42 braised rice with mushrooms; risotto

43 brindisi

44 béchamel — macaroni cheese;   tomato — spaghetti napolitaine;   demi-glace — spaghetti bolognaise

45 e.g. spaghetti, macaroni, tagliatelle, lasagne, riccioli

Questions in depth ● Outline answers . . . .

Eggs

1 a. make use of pasteurised whole eggs and cook the eggs through

   b. high temperature, overcooking, release iron, sulphur   *p181 PC*

2 a. omelette, boiled, scrambled, in cocotte, sur le plat, poached

> Ham omelette
> *Omelette au Jambon*
>
> Poached eeggs with spinach and cheese sauce
> *Oeufs pochés florentine*
>
> Scrambled eggs with kidneys
> *Oeufs brouillées aux rognons*
>
> Eggs in a cocotte with creamed chicken
> *Oeufs en cocotte à la reine*
>
> Eggs on a dish with bacon
> *Oeufs sur le plat au lard*
>
> Soft boiled eggs with sweetcorn and cheese sauce
> *Oeufs mollets Washington*

   eggs contain most nutrients, low in calories, egg protein is complete and easily digestible

   b. beaten eggs lightly cooked in butter over gentle heat stirring continuously

overcooking toughens the protein and eggs discolour by
release of iron and sulphur, syneresis occurs   *p178 PC*

c. top quality, fresh eggs broken into gently simmering water
with a little vinegar   *p183 PC*

d. beaten, seasoned eggs lightly but swiftly cooked in a special
pan then carefully shaped
folded — mushroom
filled — tomato
flat — Spanish   *p187/8 PC*

Farinaceous

3   a. i. filled pasta envelopes;   ii. filled pasta rolls;   iii. layered
sheets of pasta with a filling;   iv. braised beef, spinach,
onion, garlic, seasoning, herbs   *p197/8 PC*

b. long grain e.g. riz pilaff aux champignons — sweated onion,
rice
mushrooms cooked in stock in oven
pilaff cooked in oven, all stock added at once
risotto cooked on stove, stock gradually added during
cooking   *p202 PC*

FISH
(Chapter 10)

Short Questions . . . .

1   Give three examples of white fish.

2   Which is the odd one and why: halibut; hake; herring; or haddock?

3   Name three shellfish.

4   List five quality points for fish.

5   Which is suitable for boiling: sprats; sole; salmon; or herring?

6   Explain how fish are boiled.

7   What is a court bouillon: royal stock; boiling kettle; fish stock; or liquid for cooking oily fish?

8   What are the ingredients used in the making of a court bouillon?

9   Explain how fish are poached.

10 What term is applied to shallow fried fish: sauté; goujons; darne; or meunière?

11 What is the reason for selecting a specific side to be cooked first when shallow-frying fillets of fish: appearance is better; cooks more evenly; cooks more quickly; or portion looks larger?

12 Which side of a fillet is placed in the fat first when being shallow fried?

13 Describe three coatings for deep fried fish and explain the reason for coating fish before deep frying.

14 List seven French terms for the cuts of fish with the gender (le or la).

15 Name and describe each cut of fish from Question 14 in English.

16 How much fish is allowed per portion? On the bone; Off the bone

17 Fish velouté is used for: fish stock; fish glaze; fish sauces; or fish cocktail

18 What is the base for a sabayon: uncooked yolks; cooked whites; cooked whole eggs; or uncooked whole eggs?

19 Why may a sabayon be used in a fish sauce?

20 How is a sabayon made?

21 What care must be taken when making a sabayon?

22 Which flat fish is skinned before being filleted?

23 How would fillets of plaice meunière be finished for serving?

24 What is garnish belle meunière?

shrimp, tomato, herring roe; mushrooms, tomato, shrimp; mushrooms, shrimps, herring roe; mushrooms, tomato, herring roe

25 Match the French name with the correct ingredient in English for three variations of poisson meunière:

Grenobloise   cucumber
Doria   shrimps and sliced mushrooms
Bretonne   lemon segments and capers

26 Explain the preparation of herring for grilling.

27 How should grilled fish be finished and presented for service?

28 Mustard sauce would be served with: soused herrings; grilled herrings; shallow fried herrings; or deep fried herrings

29 How does the preparation of grilled fish St Germain differ from that of other fish?

30 A fish dish garnished with banana is called: Colére; Caprice; Colbert; or Cardinal

31 Name three raising agents that may be used in frying batters.

32 Compile a list of six points to ensure safety when deep frying fish.

33 Describe how deep fried fish is served.

34 Which sauce may be served with crumbed deep fried fish?

   egg; tartar; parsley; demi glace

35 How are whiting prepared for frying?

36 What size are filets de sole en goujons and why are they so called?

37 The marinade for fried fish à l'Orly consists of:

38 The temperature of the fat in which whitebait are cooked is:

   105°C; 125°C; 175°C; 195°C

39 Whitebait are served with their heads on: true/false.

40 What is the English term for young turbot?

41 The French for young turbot is: turbotin; truite; thon; or turbot

42 Describe the difference between brill and turbot.

43 When turbot is cut on the bone what is it called?

   darne; suprême; tronçon; goujon

44 Is it correct to write on the menu 'filet de turbot'? Yes/no.

45 Explain the reasons for the answer to Question 45.

46 What is the name given to a cut of salmon on the bone?

   tronçon; suprême; filet; darne

47   Which of the following accompanies hot cooked salmon?

sliced cucumber;   grated cheese;   grated carrot;   sliced truffle

48   Name 3 white fish which may be used for boiling.

49   When cooking whole fish in a liquid, why should the liquid be only allowed to simmer gently?

50   When poaching fish why is only the minimum of liquid used?

51   What is served with a fish dish named Véronique?

bananas;   oranges;   grapes;   apples

52   a.   What ingredients are used for cooking fish Bercy?

b.   What is added to it to become bonne femme?

c.   What is added to bonne femme to become Bréval (d'Antin)?

53   Which of the following are glazed: filets de sole vin blanc; filets de sole Bercy;   filets de sole Marguery;   or filets de sole Bréval

54   Which of the following are gratinated: filets de sole Mornay; filets de sole florentine;   filets de sole Walewska;   or filets de sole d'Antin?

55   What is kedgeree?

56   Which fish is sometimes served with black butter and capers?

halibut;   plaice;   skate;   salmon

57   What method of cookery is employed for cooking the dish in Question 56?

58   Suggest three ways of using cooked fish.

59   Mayonnaise de saumon and salade de saumon are served differently; explain how they are served.

60   If half a lobster is served for a portion, a 1kg (2lb) lobster would
     be ordered: true/false.

61   Explain the significance of using the words *fillet* and *fillets* on
     the menu.

62   How should mussels be prepared prior to cooking?

     salted and drained;   washed and filleted;   blanched and
     drained;   scraped and washed

63   Why should the raw mussel shells be tightly closed?

64   How may scallop shells be opened: on top of the stove;   in
     boiling water;   under the salamander;   or in a steamer?

65   What sort of potato is piped round the edge of a scallop shell for
     scallop with cheese sauce: mashed;   duchess;   purée;   or
     creamed?

Questions in depth . . . .

1   a. What are the two main groups of fish, give three examples
         for each and outline their respective food value.

     b. When purchasing, what are the signs of quality to look for?

     c. Name the two main groups of shellfish with three examples
         of each.

     d. What is the difference in method between skinning plaice
         fillets and Dover sole? Give two popular menu examples for
         the use of each.

2   a. Name seven ways of cooking fish and give a menu example
         for each.

     b. Give examples of liquids in which fish can be boiled or
         poached, the ingredients for a court-bouillon for oily fish and
         name six cuts of fish together with a description of each.

     c. What is the chief purpose of coating fish before deep frying,
         name three different coatings and examples of fish cooked by
         each.

     d. Give procedure for baking fish and give two menu examples.

3   a. Give method for shallow frying fish and suggest three
         variations as they would appear on a menu. Why is it
         essential to fry presentation side first?

     b. What is the difference between the preparation for;
         i. grilling herring;   ii. mackerel;   iii. fish St Germain and
         fish caprice?

     c. What would be the approximate difference in temperature
         °C between deep frying a Dover sole and whitebait and why?

     d. Suggest three hot dishes which include the use of cooked fish
         and potato.

Short Questions ● Answers . . . .

1   e.g. plaice, cod, whiting

2   herring because it is an oily fish, the others are white

3   e.g. crab, mussels, prawns

4   eyes bright, gills red, flesh firm, plentiful scales, smell   *p208 PC*

5   salmon

6   immersed in liquid and gently simmered   *p209 PC*

7   liquid for cooking oily fish

8   water, vegetables, herbs, seasoning, vinegar   *p224 PC*

9   fish barely covered with fish stock and buttered paper, gently
     brought to the boil, cooked in oven or steamer   *p209 PC*

10   meunière

11   appearance is better

12   presentation side

13   batter;   milk and flour;   flour;   egg and crumb;
     to prevent fat penetrating into fish   *p210 PC*

14 la darne; le tronçon; le filet; le suprême; le délice; les
   goujons; les goujonnettes; la paupiette

15 e.g. la darne — slice of round fish on bone
         la paupiette — stuffed and rolled fish fillet   *p211 PC*

16 on bone 150g (6oz); off bone 100g (4oz)

17 fish sauces

18 uncooked yolks   *p213 PC*

19 to enrich and assist glazing

20 whisking egg yolks and water over gentle heat   *p213 PC*

21 not to overcook or scramble the eggs

22 Dover sole

23 lemon juice, nut brown butter, parsley

24 mushrooms, tomato, herring roe

25 Grenobloise — lemon segments and capers
   Doria — cucumber; Bretonne — shrimps and mushrooms

26 descale, clean, wash, dry, incise, flour, oil   *p217 PC*

27 garnish with lemon, picked parsley, accompanying
   sauce   *p217 PC*

28 grilled herrings

29 filleted, passed through melted butter and
   breadcrumbs   *p218 PC*

30 Caprice

31 yeast, beaten egg whites (air); beaten eggs (air)

32 e.g. not overfilling fryer; dry food; not overloading fryer
         with food; careful handling   *p70 PC*

33 garnish with picked parsley, lemon and/or suitable
  sauce   *p221 PC*

34 tartar

35 picked, washed, drained, floured   *p222 PC*

36 size approx 8cm×½cm (3in×¼in) — named after a small fish
  called gudgeon

37 oil, lemon juice, chopped parsley, seasoning

38 195°C

39 true

40 chicken turbot

41 turbotin

42 turbot is almost round, brill elongated

43 tronçon

44 no

45 because a turbot fillet would be too large, it would be cut into
  portions known as suprêmes

46 darne

47 sliced cucumber

48 turbot, brill, cod

49 otherwise the fish may break up

50 to conserve flavour in the cooking liquid which is used in the
  coating sauce

51 grapes

52 a. chopped shallots, parsley, white wine, lemon, yolks,
        cream   *p228 PC*

    b. sliced button mushrooms

    c. mushrooms, tomato concassée   *p228/9 PC*

53 Bercy and Bréval

54 Mornay, florentine, Walewska

55 pilaf rice, flaked fish, hard boiled eggs, curry sauce *p231 PC*

56 skate

57 cooked in court bouillon

58 fish cakes, pie, bouchées

59 mayonnaise of salmon is coated with sauce
    salad of salmon, sauce served separately

60 false, usually half a ½kg, 1lb lobster

61 fillet should indicate one piece of fish;   fillets should indicate
    two or more

62 scraped and washed

63 because this signifies they are alive. When dead the shells open
    and should be discarded.

64 on top of the stove

65 duchess

Questions in depth • Outline answers . . . .

1   a. white e.g. plaice (flat) cod (round)
        oily e.g. mackerel
        Fish, good protein equal to meat. Oily fish vitamins A and D
        in flesh — in certain white fish, only in liver
        e.g. cod   *p207 PC*

    b. eyes, gills, flesh, scales, smell   *p208 PC*

    c. crustacea e.g. crab;   mollusca e.g. mussels   *p208 PC*

    d. plaice filleted before skinning
        sole skinned before filleting
        e.g. fried fillets of plaice, tartare sauce
              fillets of sole bonne-femme   *p208 PC*

2   a. boiling, poaching, steaming, grilling, shallow frying, deep
        frying, baking

> Grilled salmon, herb sauce
> *Darne de saumon grillé*
> *sauce aux herbes*
>
> River trout shallow fried
> with lemon and capers
> *Truite de rivière Grenobloise*
>
> Deep fried fillets of plaice in batter,
> tomato sauce
> *Filet de plie à l'Orly*
> *sauce tomates*
>
> Poached turbot,
> egg and butter sauce
> *Tronçon de turbot poché*
> *sauce Hollandaise*

    b. e.g. water and milk — fish stock
              water, vinegar, vegetables, herbs

        e.g. darne — slice of round fish on bone
              tronçon — slice of flat fish on bone   *p210 PC*

    c. to prevent fat penetration e.g. flour, egg and breadcrumbs —
        fried breadcrumbed fillets of sole — filets de sole à l'Anglaise
        milk and flour — devilled whitebait — blanchailles frits
        batter — fried fillet of codling, tartar sauce   *p210 PC*

    d. baked whole, portioned or filleted with a savoury stuffing,
        cooked in ovenproof dish with vegetables, herbs
        e.g. baked sea bass

3 a. flour, shallow fry both sides finish with lemon, parsley, nut
      brown butter
      e.g. suprême de turbotin bretonne — add shrimps,
      mushrooms
      fat is clean, giving good presentation   *p215 PC*

   b. i. herring — whole, cut incision in flesh, pass through
          seasoned flour

      ii. mackerel — opened and boned, pass through seasoned
          flour

      iii. fish St Germain — filleted, passed through seasoned
           flour, melted butter and breadcrumbs, grilled, served
           with béarnaise sauce

      iv. fish caprice — as for St Germain served with fried banana
          and sauce Robert

   c. 20°C; whitebait being much smaller require hotter fat as
      they cook more quickly

   d. e.g. fish cakes, fish pie   *p230/1/2 PC*

LAMB AND MUTTON
(Chapter 11)

Short Questions . . . .

1   Approximately how much lamb on the bone and how much off the bone is calculated per head when ordering?

2   What is the difference between lamb and mutton?

3   Name the joints in a carcass of lamb.

4   List the points which indicate quality in lamb.

5   List the small cuts of lamb.

6   State from which joints the small cuts are obtained.

7   The tail end of the saddle is called the . . .

8   A saddle divided into two lengthwise produces two . . .

9   When skinning a saddle it is best to skin from tail to head and back to breast: true/false.

10   Why is the surface of the saddle of lamb scored?

   for ease of carving;   to allow fat to flow out;   to shorten cooking time;   to assist basting

11   How is a noisette of lamb prepared?

12   List the offal obtained from a carcass of lamb.

13   Which joints of lamb may be cooked by roasting?

14   Name two kinds of lamb chops.

15   Which lamb joints are suitable for stuffing: leg;   shoulder;   best end;   loin?

16   Which sauce is traditionally served with roast lamb?

17 Which sauce is traditionally served with roast mutton?

onion; cranberry; horseradish; apple

18 Which jelly is traditionally served with roast mutton?

cranberry; orange; quince; redcurrant

19 The best end is cut into chops: true/false.

20 List the usual ingredients in a mixed grill.

21 Describe the preparation of lamb cutlets for cutlets reform.

22 What sauce is traditionally served with boiled leg of mutton?

parsley; caper; egg; mushroom

23 From what liquor is this sauce made?

24 What is a kebab, how is it cooked, and with what is it usually served?

25 What is understood by toad in the hole?

26 Suggest three ways of serving lamb chops.

27 Name and describe four suitable garnishes for serving with noisette of lamb.

28 What is the filet mignon: the top of the leg; the equivalent joint to the nut of veal; the equivalent joint to the fillet of beef; or boned out shoulder?

29 Name four different varieties of lamb stew.

30 What do the words *navarin* and *ragoût* indicate?

31 What does 'turned' mean when applied to vegetables?

shaped like a barrel; shaken in the pan; canned vegetables; finished in butter

32 How are turned vegetables produced glacé?

33   Long grain rice is used for plain boiled rice: true/false.

34   What points distinguish high standards for plain boiled rice?

35   How is a high standard of plain boiled rice achieved?

36   List a selection of items which may accompany curried lamb.

37   Bombay Duck is roasted: true/false.

38   Describe poppadums and explain how they are cooked and served.

39   What is moussaka?

40   From what country does moussaka originate: Italy;   Russia; Turkey;   or Greece?

41   Suggest three dishes using cooked lamb.

42   Name four items of lamb offal and suggest a suitable dish for each.

43   Why must sautéd kidneys be drained after being fried?

to prevent loss of juices;   to remove strong flavour;   to increase flavour;   to shrink them

44   The garnish turbigo consists of button mushrooms and chipolatas: true/false.

45   From which joint are A cutlets, B chops obtained?

Questions in depth . . . .

1   a. What are the signs of quality in a carcass of lamb?

b. Name three prime joints suitable for roasting and three suitable for stewing. Give three menu examples of lamb stew.

c. Name three lamb joints that can be boned and stuffed. Give the recipe for a suitable stuffing.

d. Name four items of lamb offal and give a menu description for each.

2   a. When roasting lamb why should joints be raised from the roasting pan by means of a trivet? What can happen to a joint if it is carved immediately it is cooked and what is the remedy?

b. Give the methods for making roast gravy.

c. Give two names for pieces of lamb cooked on a skewer. Suggest items of food that can be along with the lamb. How may different flavours be introduced?

d. Suggest and give method for two lamb dishes prepared from cooked meat.

Short Questions ● Answers . . . .

1   on bone 150g 6oz — off bone 100g 4oz

2   lamb is under 12 months old

3   shoulder, leg, breast, middle neck, scrag end, best end   *p242 PC*

4   compact, evenly fleshed, firm lean flesh, colour of flesh and fat, bone structure   *p242 PC*

5   chops, cutlets, fillet etc.   *p244/5 PC*

6   chops from loin, chumps, cutlets from best end etc.   *p245 PC*

7   the chump end

8   loins

9   false, always skin from head to tail and breast to back

10 to allow fat to flow out

11 cut on the slant from boned loin

12 kidney, heart, liver etc.   *p247 PC*

13 leg, loin, shoulder etc.   *p242 PC*

14 loin;   chump

15 shoulder, loin

16 mint

17 onion

18 redcurrant

19 false, it is cut into cutlets

20 cutlet, kidney, sausage, bacon, tomato, mushroom   *p251 PC*

21 pass prepared cutlets through seasoned flour, eggwash and
    breadcrumbs containing chopped ham and parsley   *p252 PC*

22 caper

23 the cooking liquor from the joint

24 a. slices of meat and vegetables on a skewer;   b. grilling;
        c. rice   *p253 PC*

25 sausages or a small cut of meat cooked in Yorkshire pudding
    mixture in the oven.   *p328 PC*

26 braised;   grilled;   fried

27 e.g. Fleuriste — tomatoes filled with jardinière of vegetables
          and château potatoes
          Dubarry — balls of cauliflower Mornay and château
          potatoes   *p255 PC*

28 equivalent joint to the fillet of beef

29 e.g. Navarin, curry, Irish, blanquette

30 brown stew

31 shaped like a barrel

32 turn or cut in even pieces, cook in minimum water, finally toss
    over heat in butter   *p281 PC*

33 true

34 not overcooked, rice grains not sticking together

35 pick and wash, add to boiling salted water, stir to boil, simmer
    gently, wash well, drain on a sieve, cover with a cloth   *p257 PC*

36 e.g. chutney, desiccated coconut, diced cucumber in yoghurt,
    chopped apple, sultanas etc.   *p257 PC*

37 false, it is grilled

38 thin vegetable wafers; grilled or deep fried; served as
    accompaniment to curry dishes

39 a dish of Eastern Mediterranean origin, minced lamb,
    aubergines, tomatoes etc.   *p262 PC*

40 Greece

41 moussaka; shepherds pie; minced lamb

42 liver — fried liver and bacon
    hearts — braised lambs hearts
    kidneys — grilled kidneys and bacon
    sweetbreads — sweetbread escalopes with mushrooms

43 b. to remove strong flavour contained in the juice

44 true

45 cutlets from best end; chops from loin and chump

Questions in depth ● Outline answers . . . .

1   a. compact, evenly fleshed, lean meat — colour, texture, grain
        fat even, hard, brittle, flaky, white
        bones pink, porous   *p242 PC*

    b. roasting — leg, saddle, best end, loin
        stewing — shoulder, middle neck, breast
        e.g. lamb stew with spring vegetables — Navarin d'agneau
        aux primeurs, Irish stew

c. shoulder, breast, loin
combine chopped suet, onion, herbs, breadcrumbs and
egg   *p249 PC*

d. e.g. hearts — braised
kidneys — grilled with bacon   *p264/5/6 PC*

2   a. to stop bottom surface from frying and becoming hard
slices tend to shrink and curl — rest 10–15 mins

b. remove joint, allow sediment to settle,
strain off fat, brown sediment, deglaze with stock
simmer, season, colour, strain, degrease   *p248 PC*

c. shish kebab, lamb brochette
mushrooms, peppers (red, yellow) onion, bay leaves
marinading in oil herbs etc.   *p253 PC*

d. Shepherds pie — cooked chopped onion, minced lamb,
seasoning, sauce in a dish topped with mashed potato
browned   *p261 PC*
Moussaka — cooked chopped onions, minced lamb,
seasoning, sauce in dish, layers of aubergine, tomato,
breadcrumbs, cheese, browned or béchamel with
eggs   *p262 PC*

BEEF
(Chapter 12)

Short Questions . . . .

1 Name the joints in a hindquarter of beef.

2 Name the joints in a forequarter of beef.

3 List the points of quality in beef.

4 Suggest a suitable order for dissecting a hindquarter.

5 What is brine?

6 What is brine used for: salting silverside of beef; straining beef stock; seasoning beef stews; or shrinking string on beef?

7 Name the small cuts of beef obtained from sirloin.

8 Name the four cuts on a fillet of beef.

9 Name the offal obtained from a carcass of beef.

10 Which is the most suitable joint for roasting: silverside; chuck steak; thick flank; or sirloin?

11 What are the traditional accompaniments for roast beef?

12 State the points which indicate when a joint of beef is cooked.

13 Which vegetables are served with French style boiled beef?

14 Which two items usually accompany boiled beef French style?

    capers and coarse salt; pickled red cabbage and French mustard; pickled gherkins and coarse salt; pickled gherkins and French mustard

15 Name six steaks and state from which joint they are obtained.

16 Name four degrees of grilling steaks in both English and French.

17   What is the usual garnish served with grilled steak?

18   Roast gravy is served with grilled meat: true/false.

19   Garnish Henry IV comprises: watercress and pommes pont neuf;   watercress and pommes frites;   watercress and pommes pailles;   watercress and pommes allumettes

20   A point steak is cut from the: sirloin;   wing rib;   fillet;   rump

21   Suggest four ways of serving sautéd tournedos.

22   Why is a brown beef stew served in an entrée dish?

23   Which of the following would be used in a beef stew with red wine: hock;   chablis;   claret;   or marsala?

24   Which of the following cuts would be used for beef Stroganoff?
          fillet;   topside;   thick flank;   sirloin

25   Why is this cut chosen for beef Stroganoff?

26   Which of the following is an ingredient for carbonnade of beef?
          vichy water;   wine;   beer;   cider

27   Which of the following is used in goulash?
          paprika;   pimento;   cayenne;   cinnamon

28   Goulash is garnished with gnocchi: true/false.

29   Before serving paupiettes the . . . must be removed.

30   What is the English for paupiettes de boeuf?

31   Name two cuts of beef suitable for braising.

32   Braised beef is cut with the grain or across the grain?

33   What is the reason for the answer to Question 32?

34   How is a joint of braised beef tested to see if it is cooked?

35 Suggest three suitable garnishes for braised beef.

36 Which paste is used for making dumplings?

suet; short; choux; noodle

37 How may minced beef be presented in an attractive manner?

38 Which kind of meat is used to make Vienna steaks?

lean minced beef; lean minced lamb; cooked meat;
venison

39 Croquettes, cutlets, and Vienna steaks; which is the correct
shape for each?

40 Which wine is usually added to the sauce served with braised ox
tongue? Madeira; Marsala; sherry; or port

41 An ox tongue will cook in approximately: 1–2 hours; 2–3
hours; 3–4 hours; 4–5 hours

42 Braised ox liver requires approx . . . hours simmering to become
tender.

43 400g (1lb) of tripe to 200g (½lb) onions are needed to produce
four portions: true/false.

44 Which pulse is sometimes used to garnish oxtail? lentils;
butter beans; haricot beans; or yellow split peas

45 What is the approximate cooking time for oxtail?

46 What is the price of fillet of beef?

47 What is the cost of oxtail?

48 Is ox liver more expensive than lamb's liver?

49 How much does minced beef cost?

50 Which fish could be used as an additional variation in steak and
kidney pudding?

Questions in depth . . . .

1   a. Name the points of quality to look for in beef?

   b. Excluding the fillet, name six joints from a hindquarter of beef and give two menu examples for the use of each.

   c. i. List the cuts and various uses of a fillet of beef, and

     ii. Give two different menu examples.

   d. Describe the following: minute steak, entrecôte steak, double entrecôte steak, porterhouse and T-bone steak.

2   a. Name six items of beef offal and give a menu description for the use of each.

   b. Name the four prime roasting joints of beef, give approximate cooking times and the accompaniments.

   c. What is the essential difference between boiled beef English style and boiled beef French style, name the usual joint and additional ingredients used in the cooking of each.

   d. What do you understand by: i. beef stroganoff; ii. goulash; iii. carbonnade; iv. paupiettes; v. bitok

Short Questions • Answers . . . .

1   shin, topside, silverside, thick flank, rump, sirloin, wing ribs, thin flank, fillet   *p271 PC*

2   fore rib, middle rib, chuck rib, sticking piece, plate, brisket, leg of mutton cut, shank   *p271 PC*

3   lean meat red and marbled, firm brittle fat   *p272 PC*

4   remove rump and kidney, remove thick flank
divide loin and rump from remainder
remove fillet etc.   *p272 PC*

5   preserving solution of water, salt, saltpetre, aromates   *p273 PC*

6   salting silverside of beef

7   sirloin and fillet steaks   *p274 PC*

8   Chateaubriand, fillet, tournedos, mignon   *p275 PC*

9   tongue, heart, liver, tripe, kidney, sweetbread   *p277 PC*

10 sirloin

11 Yorkshire pudding, roast gravy, horseradish sauce

12 a little blood issuing from the meat when pressed   *p278 PC*

13 celery, leek, cabbage, onions, carrots, turnips

14 pickled gherkins;   coarse salt   *p279–80 PC*

15 rump — rump;   fillet — fillet;   point — rump;
    tournedos — fillet;   minute — sirloin;   porterhouse — sirloin

16 rare — au bleu;   underdone — saignant;   just done — à
    point;   well done — bien cuit

17 watercress, deep-fried potato, suitable sauce e.g. béarnaise

18 false — usually béarnaise, devilled sauce or parsley or garlic
    butter

19 watercress and pommes pont-neuf

20 rump

21 sauce chasseur;   mushroom sauce;   sauce bordelaise;   rossini
    — topped with fore gras, truffle, coated with madeira sauce

22 so that the meat and sauce remain compact and keep fresh and
    moist. If served on a flat dish both could dry out before being
    served

23 claret

24 fillet

25 because of its tenderness

26 beer

27   paprika

28   true

29   strings

30   beef olives

31   topside;   thick flank

32   across the grain

33   because a neater, more tender slice is achieved

34   when penetrated with a trussing needle no sign of blood should issue

35   noodles, mixed vegetables, mushrooms

36   suet

37   serve in a border of lightly browned duchess potato

38   lean minced beef

39   5 cm 2in long thick rolls (croquettes)
     round thick patties (Vienna steaks)

40   Madeira

41   3–4 hours

42   1½–2 hours

43   true

44   haricot beans

45   approx 3 hours

46   current market price

47 current market price

48 no

49 current market price

50 oysters

Questions in depth ● Outline answers . . . .

1   a. lean meat, pleasing red, flecks of fat, fat firm, brittle creamy
        white, odourless   *p272 PC*

    b. wing rib e.g. roast ribs of beef, Yorkshire pudding
        topside e.g. beef olives
        thick flank e.g. braised steaks
        shin e.g. consommé
        sirloin e.g. minute steak, garlic butter
        rump e.g. grilled rump steak, béarnaise sauce   *p270 PC*

    c. i.   Chateaubriand; fillet steak; tournedos; mignon
             (tail); fillet (joint); chain   *p276 PC*

        ii. e.g. grilled fillet   *p282 PC*

             e.g. beef Stroganoff (tail end)   *p286 PC*

    d. minute steak — thin cuts from sirloin, flattened so steak
        cooks in minute
        entrecôte steak — thicker cuts from sirloin
        double entrecôte steak — doublesize of sirloin steak
        porterhouse — cut from rib end of sirloin including bone
        T-bone steak — cut from rump end of sirloin including bone
        and fillet   *p274 PC*

2   a. heart e.g. braised ox heart; liver e.g. liver and onions;
        kidneys e.g. stewed beef kidney and mushrooms;
        sweetbreads e.g. braised veal sweetbreads with vegetables;
        tail e.g. braised oxtail; tripe e.g. tripe and onions

    b. sirloin, wing ribs, fore ribs, fillet
        approx 15 mins per lb plus 15 mins
        gravy, Yorkshire pudding, horseradish sauce

c. English — meat salted — silverside, thin or thick flank,
carrots, onions, dumplings
French — meat unsalted — brisket, onions, carrots, turnips,
celery, leeks, cabbage   *p279/80 PC*

d. i.   strips of beef fillet sautéd in sauce of shallots, cream,
wine, lemon served with pilaff rice   *p286 PC*

ii. traditional Hungarian dish stewed beef flavoured
paprika   *p287 PC*

iii. traditional Belgian dish of thin steaks stewed in beer with
onions, sugar and tomato   *p289 PC*

iv. thin slices of beef, stuffed and braised — beef
olives   *p292 PC*

v.   fried patties of lean minced beef, onion, egg and
breadcrumbs   *p294 PC*

VEAL
(Chapter 13)

Short Questions . . . .

1   Name the joints in a carcass of veal.

2   The average weight of a Dutch milk fed leg of veal is:

9–12kg (18–24lb);   15–18kg (30–36lb);   21–24kg (42–48lb)

3   The proportion of bone in a leg of veal is approximately:

7%;   14%;   21%;   28%

4   The proportion of meat in a leg of veal suitable for escalopes is:

20%;   30%;   36%;   46%

5   Which of the following is used for osso buco: leg;   loin;   breast;   or knuckle?

6   Calves' liver is one of the most suitable livers for frying: true/false.

7   The corresponding veal joint to topside of beef is . . .

8   The corresponding veal joint of silverside of beef is . . .

9   The corresponding veal joint to thick flank of beef is . . .

10   When dissecting a leg of veal, the knuckle is removed first: true/false.

11   The anticipated yield of 100g (4oz) escalopes from a 18kg (36lb) leg of veal would be:

65;   55;   45;   35

12   What colour is the flesh of good quality veal?

13   Flesh of good quality veal should be firm in structure, not soft or flabby: true/false.

14   When preparing osso buco, shin of veal should be cut:

    2–3cm (1–1½in);   1–1½cm (½–¾in);   3–4cm (1½–2in);
    4–6cm (2–3in)

15   Why should veal sweetbreads be well washed, blanched, and trimmed before being used?

16   A brown veal stew is known as: ragoût;   navarin;   blanquette;   fricassée

17   For a blanquette of veal the meat is cooked in stock: true/false.

18   For a fricassée of veal, the meat is cooked in sauce: true/false.

19   Any white stew of veal may be finished with a liaison of

20   A fricassée of veal may be finished by adding a few drops of lemon juice: true/false.

21   Garnish à l'ancienne consists of:

    button onions and button mushrooms;   button onions and lardons;   button onions and tomatoes;   button onions and courgettes

22   Which of the following pastes would you use to cover a hot veal and ham pie: short;   rough puff or puff;   hot water;   or choux?

23   When preparing a stuffing for veal olives, the finely chopped meat trimmings can be added: true/false.

24   The best veal escalopes are cut from the . . . or . . . of veal?

25   Which of the following is most suitable for frying veal escalopes?   lard;   margarine;   olive oil;   or oil and butter

26   Which of the following veal escalopes would be garnished with a fried egg and anchovy fillets?   viennoise;   à la crème;   napolitaine;   or Holstein

27   Veal escalopes with cream are pané (flour, egg and crumbed): true/false.

28 Veal escalopes with Madeira are lightly floured before cooking: true/false.

29 What additions are usually made when roasting a leg of veal in order to increase flavour?

30 Roast gravy served with veal is traditionally: thin; or thickened

31 Traditional garnish with roast leg of veal is:

> parsley and thyme stuffing and thinly sliced ham
> sage and onion stuffing and thinly sliced ham
> parsley and chive stuffing and chipolata sausage
> parsley and thyme stuffing and chipolata sausage

32 Veal stuffing traditionally contains chopped suet: true/false.

33 Which of the following is more traditionally used in the cooking of osso buco: Marsala; red wine; Madeira; or dry white wine?

34 Which of the following is usually served with calf's liver and bacon: tomato sauce; mustard sauce; devilled sauce; or jus lié?

35 What are sweetbreads and what are their proper names?

> glands; muscles; nerves; joints

36 Which sweetbread is of superior quality: throat; or stomach?

37 Veal sweetbreads may be braised white or brown: true/false.

38 Which would be considered a suitable garnish for fried breadcrumbed veal escalopes: stuffed tomatoes; grilled bacon; aubergine provençale; or asparagus tips?

Questions in depth . . . .

1   a. What are the points of quality in a carcass of veal and what is an average weight for a leg of prime milk-fed veal?

   b. Give a menu example for use of each of the following veal joints/cuts: knuckle, leg, best-end, shoulder.

c. What is the essential difference between a fricassée and a blanquette of veal? Give the ingredients and method for Fricassée de veau à l'ancienne and suggest suitable vegetable accompaniments.

d. i. Name two suitable veal joints for stuffing and roasting and

   ii. give ingredients and method for a veal stuffing.

2 a. From which joint in a carcass of veal are the best escalopes obtained? Approximately how many 4oz escalopes could be obtained from a 36lb leg?

b. Describe the preparation and serving of three popular breadcrumbed veal escalopes.

c. What is the difference in preparation between a veal escalope for Viennoise and à la crème? What alcoholic liquor can be used to flavour the cream sauce? What is the most simple variation to veal escalope à la crème?

d. i. What are sweetbreads?

   ii. Which two types are used for cooking?

   iii. Which of the two is superior in quality and describe its shape?

   iv. Name and describe three ways of cooking sweetbreads.

   v. What is a veal pojarski?

Short Questions • Answers ....

1   cushion, under cushion, thick flank, knuckle, shoulder, loin, best end, neck-end, scrag   *p302 PC*

2   21–24kg (42–48lb)

3   14%

4   46%

5   knuckle

6   true

7   cushion

8   under cushion

9   thick flank

10 true

11 $55 \times 100g$ (4oz)

12 pale pink

13 true

14 2–3cm (1–1½ins) thick

15 to thoroughly cleanse them

16 ragoût

17 true

18 true

19 egg yolks and cream

20 true

21 button onions and button mushrooms

22 hot water

23 true

24 cushion or under cushion

25 oil and butter

26 d. Holstein

27 false, they are lightly flavoured

28 true

29 bed of roots and sprigs of thyme and rosemary

30 thickened

31 parsley and thyme stuffing and thinly sliced ham

32 true

33 d. dry white wine

34 d. jus lié

35 glands, thymus and pancreas glands

36 stomach (heart shaped)

37 true

38 asparagus tips

Questions in depth ● Outline answers . . . .

1   a. flesh, pale pink, firm, not flabby
        cut surfaces slightly moist, pinkish bones
        firm, pinkish white fat, firm well covered kidney

        18kg 36lbs;   23kg 46lbs   *p304 PC*

    b. e.g. osso bucco, cuissot de veau rôtie, roast stuffed shoulder
        of veal

    c. meat cooked in stock — blanquette
        meat cooked in sauce — fricassée
        for fricassée — set meat in butter without colour, mix in
        flour, cook out, add stock
        when cooked, pick out meat, add sabayon to sauce, lemon
        juice
        finish parsley, croûtons, button onions and mushrooms
        fricassée de veau à l'ancienne, riz pilaff, haricots
        verts   *p306 PC*

    d. i.   shoulder, breast

        ii. cooked onions, suet, herbs, breadcrumbs   *p313 PC*

2   a. cushion or nut from the leg;   55   *p303 PC*

    b. e.g. escalope de veau viennoise — breadcrumbed
thinly battened-out slice of veal — flour, egg, crumbed,
shallow fried, finished slice of lemon, capers, chopped
parsley, egg, nut-brown butter

    c. Viennoise — flour, egg, crumbed;   à la crème — floured
e.g. white wine, sherry
add mushrooms   *p312 PC*

    d. i.   glands

        ii.   thymus, pancreas

        iii. pancreas, heart-shaped

        iv.   e.g. Ris de veau braisé (à blanc)
Wash, blanch, refresh sweetbreads. Cook in covered pan
on bed of roots, herbs and stock. Remove lid when three
quarters cooked, baste frequently to glaze.   *p316 PC*

        v.   minced veal, egg, cream, breadcrumbs moulded cutlet
shape shallow fried   *p314 PC*

PORK AND BACON
(Chapter 14)

Short Questions . . . .

1 Name the joints in a side of pork.

2 The lean flesh of good quality pork should be pale pink, soft and of a fine texture: true/false.

3 In order to be able to carve a leg of pork efficiently, it is not necessary to remove the aitch bone before the leg is cooked: true/false.

4 When scoring the rind of pork, how far apart should the incisions be?

   2mm (⅛in);   1cm (½in);   2cm (1in);   3cm(1½in)

5 Which of the following herbs is most suitable for seasoning a boned, rolled belly of pork for roasting: thyme;   parsley;   tarragon;   or sage?

6 In an oven at 230–250°C a leg of pork should be roasted for approximately:

   10 minutes to the ½kg (1lb) and 10 minutes over
   15 minutes to the ½kg (1lb) and 15 minutes over
   20 minutes to the ½kg (1lb) and 20 minutes over
   25 minutes to the ½kg (1lb) and 25 minutes over

7 Roast pork must always be well cooked: true/false.

8 The traditional accompaniments for roast pork are:

   roast gravy, orange sauce, sage and onion stuffing
   roast gravy, apple sauce, parsley and thyme stuffing
   roast gravy, prune sauce, sage and parsley stuffing
   roast gravy, apple sauce, sage and onion stuffing

9 Traditionally, sage and onion stuffing should be prepared using dripping from the pork joint: true/false.

10 Is a dish of pease-pudding suitable for serving with boiled pork? Yes/no.

11 Which of the following sauces is most suitable for serving with a grilled pork chop? tomato; apple; parsley; or tartar

12 Which of the following would be cooked in with a dish of pork chops à la flamande? red cabbage; peas; apples; or tomatoes

13 Which of the following pork joints is most suitable for barbecues? spare ribs; loin; shoulder; or leg

14 Forcemeat is a term given to: numerous mixtures of meats; sausage meat before putting into skins; stuffing for roast pork joints; a mince made from a meat substitute

15 What is the price of a leg of pork per ½kg (1lb)?

16 What is the price of shoulder of pork per ½kg (1lb)?

17 What is the price of loin of pork per ½kg (1lb)?

18 What is the price of spare rib of pork per ½kg (1lb)?

19 Name the joints on a side of bacon.

20 What is the price of prime gammon per ½kg (1lb)?

21 What is the price of back rashers per ½kg (1lb)?

22 What is the price of streaky bacon per ½kg (1lb)?

23 The approximate weight of a gammon is:

    2½kg (5lb);   5kg (10lb);   7½kg (15lb);   10kg (20lb)

24 In assessing quality, the lean of bacon should be a deep pink colour and firm: true/false.

25 In assessing quality, the fat should be white, smooth and not excessive in proportion to the lean: true/false.

26 What is the most popular cut of bacon for frying: collar; hock;   or streaky?

27 Gammon rashers for grilling should be cut as thinly as possible: true/false.

28 When preparing hock of bacon for boiling, in order to facilitate carving, it is best to leave all bones in: true/false.

29 What should be considered before soaking a bacon joint before boiling.

30 When boiling bacon allow per ½kg (1lb):

> 10 minutes + 10 minutes over;   15 minutes + 15 minutes over;   20 minutes + 20 minutes over;   25 minutes + 25 minutes over

31 Boiled bacon should be removed from the cooking liquor as soon as it is cooked: true/false.

32 What is the traditional sauce for serving with hot boiled bacon?

> tomato;   apple;   chestnut;   parsley

33 Which of the following accompaniments is most traditional for serving with hot boiled bacon: macaroni cheese;   mashed turnips;   buttered swede;   pease-pudding?

34 Grilled gammon rashers should only be served for breakfast: true/false.

35 In order to carve a ham efficiently and help to keep the slices intact, it is better to leave the aitch bone in: true/false.

36 Which of the following hams is so prepared that it can be sliced thinly and eaten raw: Polish;   Danish;   Wiltshire;   or Parma?

37 A ham is cut from a side of pork: true/false.

38 A gammon is cut from a side of pork: true/false.

Questions in depth . . . .

1 a. Name the quality points in pork, name four joints suitable
for roasting and give approximate age and weight for a
suckling pig.

b. i. Give approximate time for roasting pork.

ii. How can the skin be kept crisp and what is the name
given to the skin?

iii. What are the traditional accompaniments to roast pork?

iv. Give ingredients and method for sage and onion stuffing.

c. i. What are the quality points for bacon?

ii. Name the three prime joints for cutting rashers.

d. Give the preparation and method for boiling bacon, name
three suitable joints and give a menu example.

Short Questions ● Answers . . . .

1 leg, loin, spare rib, belly, shoulder, head   *p322 PC*

2 true

3 false, removal of the aitchbone assists carving

4 2cm 1in

5 sage

6 25 mins to the lb plus 25 mins

7 true

8 roast gravy, apple sauce, sage and onion stuffing

9 true

10 yes

11 apple

12 red cabbage

13   spare ribs

14   numerous mixture of minced meats   *p328 PC*

15   current market prices (find this out)

16   current market prices   ”

17   current market prices   ”

18   current market prices   ”

19   collar, hock, back, streaky, gammon   *p331 PC*

20   current market prices (find this out)

21   current market prices   ”

22   current market prices   ”

23   7½kg 15lbs

24   true

25   true

26   streaky

27   false, they should be cut in fairly thick slices

28   false, bones hinder efficient carving

29   the salt content

30   25 mins per lb plus 25 mins

31   false, it should be left to cool in the cooking liquid

32   parsley

33   pease-pudding

34   false, they can be served for any meal

35   false, neater slices are obtained if aitch bone is removed

36   Parma

37   true

38   false, it is cut from a side of bacon

Questions in depth ● Outline answers . . . .

1   a.   lean flesh pale pink, firm, fine texture or grain, rind smooth
     leg, loin, spare rib, shoulder
     5–6 weeks;   10–20lbs   *p322 PC*

    b.   i.   25 minutes per lb and 25 minutes over

         ii.   brushing with oil;   crackling

         iii. roast gravy, apple sauce, sage and onion stuffing

         iv.   chopped onions cooked in pork dripping, herbs and
               white breadcrumbs   *p325 PC*

    c.   i.   not sticky;   clean smell;   smooth rind
              lean meat deep pink and firm, fat — white and
              smooth   *p331 PC*

         ii.   back;   belly (streaky);   gammon

    d.   soak in cold water if necessary
         change water, simmer until cooked, cool in liquid
         e.g. boiled bacon, pease-pudding, parsley sauce   *p333 PC*

POULTRY AND GAME
(Chapter 15)

Short Questions . . . .

1   The largest chicken suitable for roasting is a capon: true/false.

2   The approximate weight of a baby chicken (poussin) is:

    200g (½lb);   ½kg (1lb);   1kg (2lb);   1½kg (3lb)

3   List four signs of quality in chicken.

4   What is the price of prime roasting chicken per ½kg (1lb)?

5   What is the price of old boiling fowl per ½kg (1lb)?

6   When preparing a chicken for roasting the wishbone may be removed in order to facilitate carving: true/false.

7   The traditional method of cutting a chicken into pieces for sauté yields 2 drumsticks, 2 thighs, 2 wings, 2 breasts and the carcass: true/false.

8   The most suitable weight of chicken for cutting suprême is:

    ¾–1kg (1½–2lb);   1¼–1½kg (2½–3lb);   2–3kg (4–6lb)

9   When preparing suprêmes of chicken is the skin left: on;   off?

10   Why is it more efficient to remove the wishbone from a chicken before removing the suprêmes?

11   A ballottine is:

    a boned stuffed leg of chicken;   a ball shaped chicken cutlet;   a brown stew of chicken legs;   a kitchen knife for cutting ball shaped pieces

12   List four signs of quality in ducks.

13   What is the price of prime duck per ½kg (1lb)?

14   What is the approximate weight of a goose?

    2kg (4lb);   3kg (6lb);   4kg (8lb);   6kg (12lb)

15 Turkeys are available in weights from 3½–20kg (7–40lb): true/false.

16 Which is the traditional stuffing for turkey?

> breadcrumbs and parsley
> forcemeat and sage
> sausage meat and chestnuts
> breadcrumbs and chestnuts

17 Which are the traditional accompaniments for roast turkey?

> roast gravy, bread sauce, cranberry sauce, chipolatas, bacon
> roast gravy, white sauce, apple sauce, sausage, ham
> roast gravy, parsley sauce, tomato sauce, chipolatas, bacon
> roast gravy, bread sauce, cranberry sauce, ham, bacon

18 Which of the following weights of raw dressed bird are required to yield four good portions of raw chicken?

> ¾–1kg (1½–2lb);   1¼–1½kg (3lb);   ½–¾kg (1–1½lb);
> 2–2½kg (4–5lb)

19 When a roast chicken is cooked there should be slight signs of blood in the juice issuing from it: true/false.

20 When preparing a stuffing for roast chicken the chopped raw chicken liver may be added: true/false.

21 What ingredients are used to make the devil mixture for grilled devilled chicken?

22 Is a chicken spatchcock: boiled; fried; roast; or grilled?

23 When preparing a jus-lié or demi-glace for use with a chicken sauté, the chicken giblets should not be used as they may taint the sauce: true/false.

24 Which of the following are typical ingredients of chicken sauté chasseur?

> mushrooms, bacon, tomatoes
> tomatoes, courgettes, parsley
> mushrooms, tomatoes, tarragon
> tomatoes, rice, tarragon

25   When cooking pieces of chicken for a sauté, indicate with numbers 1–4 the order they are put into the pan. Give the reason: thighs; drumsticks; wings; breasts

26   When cooking suprême de volaille à la créme, the suprêmes should be lightly floured and cooked in butter with the minimum amount of colour: true/false.

27   When preparing suprême de volaille aux pointes d'asperges it is usual to pané the suprêmes: true/false.

28   Which of the following rice dishes is usually served with boiled chicken and suprême sauce?

   risotto with short grain rice;   risotto with long grain rice; pilaf with short grain rice;   pilaf with long grain rice

29   Which of the following are typical of chicken à la king?

   red pimento, mushrooms, marsala;   green pimento, mushrooms, red wine;   red pimento, mushrooms, sherry; green pimento, mushrooms, white wine

30   When preparing chicken vol-au-vent, the chicken mixture should be put into the puff pastry cases well in advance of service in order to let the flavour soak into the pastry: true/false.

31   Chicken cutlets must always be deep fried: true/false.

32   When preparing a fricassée of chicken, the pieces of chicken should be cooked in with the sauce: true/false.

33   Which of the following are the more usual ingredients in a chicken pie?

   mushroom, bacon, hard-boiled egg, parsley
   onions, carrots, leeks, celery
   mushrooms, carrots, hard-boiled egg, sage
   onions, rosemary, tomatoes, courgettes

34   A chicken salad would normally be accompanied by a mayonnaise sauce: true/false.

35 When preparing a curry of chicken, the curry powder should be diluted in water and added to the dish for the last few minutes of cooking only: true/false.

36 Which of the following is the traditional accompaniment to a curry of chicken?

> plain boiled rice, raw sliced mushrooms, bacon
> pilaf rice, sliced tomatoes, grated cheese
> pilaf rice, boiled ham, chutney
> plain boiled rice, grilled poppadums and Bombay duck

37 What are the traditional accompaniments for English roast duck?

> sage and onion stuffing and cranberry sauce
> thyme and parsley stuffing and cranberry sauce
> sage and onion stuffing and apple sauce
> thyme and parsley stuffing and apple sauce

38 When preparing orange salad to serve with roast duck how are the oranges cut?

> segments free from skin and pips; slices with skins and rind on; slices free from skin and pips; quarters with skin and rind on

39 It is not necessary to stone cherries for duckling with cherries: true/false.

40 Which of the following is cooked in with braised duck and peas?

> lardons, button onions, peas; ham, chipolatas, peas; lardons, chipolatas, peas; carrots, turnips, peas

41 What is venison?

42 What type of meat is venison: dry and tough; dry and tender; moist and tough; moist and tender?

43 Describe two procedures which help to overcome the dryness and toughness in venison.

44 A carcass of venison should be hung for approximately:

> 1–2 days; 5–6 days; 8–9 days; 12–21 days

45   List six vegetables and herbs used in a marinade.

46   Are the more tender joints of venison obtained from the fore or hindquarter?

47   Compare the prices of venison and beef.

48   To test for age, the ear of a young hare should tear easily between the fingers: true/false.

49   What is the price of a young hare?

50   After killing, and before cleaning, a hare should be hung for approximately:

    1–2 days;   3–4 days;   6–7 days;   10–11 days

51   A brown stew of hare is known as: ragoût;   sauté;   fricassée; civet

52   What is the traditional English term for a brown stew of hare?

53   Why is the blood saved when preparing a brown stew of hare?

54   The dish in question 53 should be garnished with:

    buttons onions, button mushrooms, lardons;   button onions, tomatoes, peas;   button onions, button mushrooms, rice;   button mushrooms, lardons, peas

55   Heart-shaped croûtons spread with redcurrant jelly should also garnish the dish: true/false.

56   Give the English translation for the following:

    faisan;   perdreau;   canard sauvage;   bécasse;   bécassine

57   How can the flavour of most game birds be improved before preparing and cooking them?

58   What happens to the flesh of game birds during the hanging process?

59   Game birds should be plucked before being hung: true/false.

60 What type of game bird should *not* be hung for too long?

61 What do we mean when we say a game bird is 'high'?

62 Name five ingredients used in making a game farce.

63 Why should you tie a piece of fat bacon over the breast of a game bird before roasting?

64 What are the traditional accompaniments to a roast game bird?

65 A partridge should be hung for:

    1–2 days;   3–5 days;   7–9 days;   10–12 days

66 Is a snipe larger or smaller than a woodcock?

67 Why is it particularly important that water game birds be eaten only in season?

68 What is a teal?

69 The grouse season is:

    August 1st–November 30th;   August 30th–December 31st;   August 12th–December 10th;   August 12th–January 31st

70 The approximate weight of a grouse is:

    150g (6oz);   300g (12oz);   400g (1lb);   600g (1½lb)

71 Hot roast grouse is normally cooked slightly underdone: True/false.

72 What is a salmis of game?

73 What were the prices of the following game when last in season?

    grouse;   pheasant;   partridge

74 Place the following in order of size from the smallest to the largest: pheasant; snipe; partridge

Questions in depth . . . .

1 a. How is a prepared raw chicken assessed for quality, what are the signs of an old bird?

   b. Describe a chicken suprême and a ballottine, give two menu examples for each.

   c. Give the average weight of a chicken to be cut for sauté, name the cut pieces, what is the order in which chicken pieces should be placed in the pan and why, give menu examples for two chicken sauté dishes.

   d. Name five hot dishes that can be prepared using cooked chicken. What do you understand by:

      i. coq au vin; ii. galantine; iii. emincé;
      iv. Parmentier; v. devilled; vi. spatchcock;
      vii. poussin?

2 a. i. What is the approximate weight variation in turkeys?

      ii. What is the approximate raw weight per portion allowed?

      iii. What preliminary preparation is required to facilitate carving of the breasts?

      iv. What pre-preparation is required for turkey legs?

      v. When roasting in an oven at 200°C–230°C reg 6–8 what is the approximate cooking time per lb?

      vi. What are the traditional accompaniments to roast turkey?

   b. i. What are the signs of quality in a duck?

      ii. What is the difference between canard and caneton?

      iii. What are the traditional accompaniments to roast duck? Give the menu descriptions for three other hot duck dishes. Describe the ingredients and service of roast duck orange salad.

   c. i. State the nature of venison.

      ii. What are the procedures for overcoming the nature of venison?

iii. State the ingredients for a venison marinade.

iv. What is the most popular way of serving hare, how is this dish thickened? and

v. What is the usual garnish?

vi. State four ways of cooking rabbit.

d. i. Name the three most popular game birds.

ii. How can the flavour of most game birds be improved?

iii. Give the reasons why?

iv. What are the signs that indicate a young game bird?

v. Why is it particularly important that water birds be eaten only in season?

vi. What is a salmis of game?

Short Questions ● Answers . . . .

1 true

2 ½kg 1lb

3 plump breast, pliable breast bone, firm flesh, unbroken skin with faint blue tint

4 current market prices

5 current market prices

6 true

7 true

8 1¼–1½kg (2½–3lb)

9 off

10 because the suprême can then be removed more cleanly and efficiently

11 a boned stuffed chicken leg

12   plump breast, pliable lower back, easily torn webbed feet, yellow feet and bill

13   current market price

14   6kg 12lbs

15   true

16   sausagemeat and chestnuts

17   roast gravy, bread sauce, cranberry sauce, chipolatas, bacon

18   1¼–1½kg (3lb)

19   true

20   true

21   mustard, Worcester sauce, cayenne pepper, vinegar

22   grilled

23   false, when properly cleaned they assist in giving flavour to a sauce

24   mushrooms, tomatoes, tarragon

25   drumsticks, thighs, wings, breasts

     In this order the toughest pieces are cooked first. If all pieces were cooked at the same time the tender pieces (wings, breast) could be overcooked.

26   true

27   true

28   pilaf with long grain rice

29   red pimento;   mushrooms;   sherry   *p360 PC*

30 false, the chicken should be placed into pre-warmed puff pastry cases at the last moment in order to keep them crisp.

31 false, they may be shallow or deep fried

32 true

33 mushroom, bacon, hard boiled egg, parsley   *p366 PC*

34 it could be, but a vinaigrette would be more usual

35 false, the curry powder should be cooked in with the chicken from the beginning   *p367 PC*

36 plain boiled rice, grilled poppadums, Bombay duck   *p257 PC*

37 sage and onion stuffing, apple sauce

38 segments free from skin and pips

39 false

40 lardons, buttons, peas   *p368 PC*

41 flesh of the deer

42 dry and tough

43 hanging the carcass for 12–21 days according to the temperature marinading in herbs, vegetables, wine, vinegar etc.   *p372 PC*

44 12–21 days

45 onions, carrots, celery, parsley, thyme, bayleaf

46 hindquarter

47 current market prices, ensure that equivalent joints of each are compared

48 true

49   current market price

50   6–7 days

51   civet

52   jugged hare

53   to thicken the sauce   *p373* **PC**

54   button onions, lardons, button mushrooms

55   true

56   pheasant, partridge, wild duck, woodcock, snipe

57   hang for a few days before plucking and eviscerating

58   the flesh slowly drains of blood, disintegration begins and
        enzyme action tenderises and develops flavour   *p376* **PC**

59   false

60   water birds   *p376* **PC**

61   it has been hung for too long and has started to give off an
        offensive odour

62   game livers, onion, thyme, bayleaf, butter   *p376* **PC**

63   to keep the flesh moist and prevent it drying out

64   roast gravy, bread sauce, brown breadcrumbs

65   3–5 days

66   smaller

67   because their oily flesh may go rancid

68   small wild duck

69   August 12–December 10

70   300g (12oz)

71   true

72   mixture of game cut into portions and cooked in a rich brown
     sauce   *p378 PC*

73   current prices

74   snipe, partridge, pheasant

Questions in depth • Outline answers . . . .

1   a. plump breast, pliable breast bone, firm flesh   *p344 PC*
       unbroken white skin, faint bluish tint
       old bird has coarse leg scales, large spurs, long hairs on skin

    b. suprême — wing and half the chicken breast with trimmed
       wing bone attached   *p357 PC*
       e.g. crumbed wing and breast of chicken with mushrooms
       ballottine — boned, stuffed leg e.g. Ballottine de volaille
       chasseur — boned, stuffed leg of chicken with tomatoes,
       mushrooms and white wine sauce

    c. 1¼–1½kg; 2½–3lbs, drumstick, wing etc.   *p345 PC*
       tougher pieces first e.g. drumstick   *p353 PC*
       e.g. Poulet sauté aux champignons

    d. Chicken vol-au-vent — Vol-au-vent de volaille
       Chicken in creamy sauce with pimentoes and glazed —
       Emincé de volaille à la king
       Chicken croquettes — Croquettes de volaille

       i.   Coq au vin — chicken in red wine   *p368 PC*

       ii. Galantine — cooked chicken; forcemeat roll, served
            cold, usually decorated for buffets   *p360 PC*

       iii. Emincé — pieces of sliced cooked chicken   *p360 PC*

       iv. Parmentier — garnish of diced fried potatoes   *p358 PC*

       v.   Devilled — devilled, usually refers to a method of grilling
            chicken   *p356 PC*

       vi. Spatchcock — method of cutting a chicken for
            grilling   *p354 PC*

     vii. Poussin — baby chicken   *p343 PC*

2   a. i.   3½–20kg (7–40lbs)

       ii.   200g–½lb

      iii. removal of wishbone

      iv. sinews drawn out of legs   *p349 PC*

       v.   15–20 mins per lb

      vi. chestnut stuffing, parsley and thyme stuffing, roast gravy, bread sauce, cranberry sauce etc.   *p350 PC*

  b. i.   e.g. plump breast, back bends easily, feet tear easily, bill yellow   *p349 PC*

       ii. fully grown duck;   duckling — young duck

      iii. e.g. gravy, apple sauce, stuffing   *p369 PC*
e.g. braised duck with peas — canard braisé aux petit pois   *p368 370/1 PC*
e.g. roasted duck, lettuce, orange zest, acidulated cream dressing   *p370 PC*
e.g. duckling with orange sauce — caneton   *p370 PC*

  c. i.   dry, tough — bigarrade

       ii. hanging, marinading   *p372 PC*

      iii. oil, vegetables, herbs, red wine

      iv. jugged thickened with blood

       v.   mushrooms, button onions, lardons, croûtons *p373 PC*

      vi. pie, curry, fricassée   *p374/5 PC*

  d. i.   pheasant; partridge; grouse

       ii. by hanging, which drains blood and begins disintegration

      iii. enzyme action then tenderises flesh and improves flavour   *p376 PC*

      iv. flexible beak, pliable breast bone, grey legs with underdeveloped spurs, pointed wing feathers

       v.   out of season flesh is coarse and fishy in taste *p377 PC*

      vi. brown ragoût of game   *p378 PC*

VEGETARIAN DISHES
(Chapter 16)

Short Questions . . . .

1 Very briefly explain the difference between a vegan and a vegetarian.

2 From what is soy sauce derived?

3 What is tofu?

4 Crudités are: crude oils; raw vegetables; oriental spices

5 Match the following:

Ratatouille	1	a source of oil
Lentils	2	a vegetable dish
Allspice	3	a pulse
Sesame seed	4	a seasoning
Smetana	5	a colouring
Saffron	6	a dairy product

6 What is tvp?

7 Name six nuts

8 Outline the method for cooking dried beans.

9 For what reasons do people become vegetarians.

10 List four vegetarian dishes suitable as a main course.

Questions in depth . . . .

1 a. Discuss the factors concerning vegetables that affect their cooking times?

   b. State the general rules for boiling vegetables, explain the reasons why some are started in cold water and others in boiling water and how the nutritive value is affected.

   c. What is the difference between the preparation of runner beans and French beans?

    d. What are the differences between the cooking for:
fresh peas;   frozen peas;   French style peas;   sugar peas
(mange-tout)

2   a. Briefly describe three different ways of cooking cabbage.
What is the effect of overcooking cabbage or any green
vegetable in relation to its food value?

    b. By which method of cookery is red cabbage usually cooked
and what ingredients may be added?

    c. What are the advantages of high speed steam cookers in
relation to batch cookery?

    d. State the quality and purchasing points of root and green
vegetables and how they should be stored.

    e. What is the difference between a vegetarian and a vegan?

Short Questions ● Answers . . . .

1 Vegetarians and vegans do not eat fish, meat, poultry or game
and vegans in addition do not consume dairy products, milk and
eggs   *p381 PC*

2 soya beans

3 low fat bean curd made from soya beans

4 raw vegetables

5 ratatouille — vegetable dish, lentils — pulse, allspice —
seasoning, sesame seed — source of oil, smetana — dairy
product, saffron — colouring

6 textured vegetable protein derived from soya beans

7 e.g. walnuts, pecans, almonds, hazelnuts, peanuts, pistachios

8 pick and wash, soak for up to 24 hours (if necessary), drain off
water, cover with fresh water, simmer gently with additional
flavouring of vegetables and herbs.

9 e.g. religion, health, choice

10   e.g. bean goulash, Caribbean fruit curry, Cornish vegetable feast
bake pie, vegetarian moussaka

Questions in depth ● Outline answers ....

1   a. age, quality, freshness, size and type   *p406 PC*

    b. root vegetables in cold, green vegetables in boiling water
       minimum cooking time retains maximum flavour, food
       value, colour   *p406 PC*

    c. side strings removed from runner beans, cut in thin strips.
       French beans topped and tailed, cut into even
       strips   *p424/5 PC*

    d. fresh peas — varied cooking times according to age,
       freshness, size
       frozen peas — consistent cooking time of short
       duration   *p428 PC*
       French style peas — cooked under cover with additional
       ingredients either on top of stove or in oven, thickened with
       beurre manié   *p428 PC*
       sugar peas — topped and tailed, cooked and served in the
       pods   *p429 PC*

2   a. i.   e.g. boiled or steamed, trim, shred, wash, cook for
          minimum time   *p415/6 PC*

       ii. stir-fried

       iii. braised, with vegetables, herbs, stock

       iv. overcooking lessens vitamin content   *p415 PC*

    b. by braising — with the addition of vinegar, apples
       etc.   *p417 PC*

    c. reduction in cooking time;   retention of flavour;   smaller
       quantities cooked as required during service   *p406 PC*

    d. root e.g. clean, firm, sound   *p124 T of C*
       green e.g. fresh;   condition of leaves;   stored — root, empty
       from sacks, store in bins, or racks   *p125 T of C*
       green — well ventilated, cool area
       salad — cool area preferably refrigerated

    e. Vegetarian does not eat any meat or fish but will eat dairy
       produce
       Vegans do not eat meat, fish or dairy produce   *p381 PC*

VEGETABLES
(Chapter 17)

Short Questions . . . .

1   Vegetables which grow above the ground should be started in boiling salted water: true/false.

2   As a general rule the cooking of all root vegetables with the exception of new potatoes is started in cold salted water: true/false.

3   Suggest a suitable sauce for serving with:

   hot globe artichoke;   cold globe artichoke

4   To cook a globe artichoke allow approximately:

   5–10 minutes;   10–15 minutes;   20–30 minutes;   40–45 minutes

5   Name the liquid in which artichokes bottoms are cooked.

6   Two types of artichoke are used in cookery. One is globe, name the other.

7   What is the current price of a globe artichoke?

8   What is the current price of a tin of artichoke bottoms?

9   How many pieces of asparagus are usually served per portion?

   2–3;   4–5;   6–8;   10–12

10 It is not necessary to wash asparagus before cooking: true/false.

11 Asparagus will cook in approximately: 5 minutes;   10 minutes;   15 minutes;   20 minutes

12 Suggest two sauces for serving with hot asparagus.

13 Asparagus is only served hot: true/false.

14 What is the approximate price of fresh asparagus per ½kg (1lb)?

15 What is an approximate price of frozen asparagus per ½kg (1lb)?

16 Young thin asparagus are known as . . .

17 The French name for egg-plant is . . .

18 What is the price of aubergines?

19 Could duxelle be used to stuff egg-plant?
      Yes/no.

20 What is ratatouille?

21 Broccoli may be cooked and served as for any cauliflower recipe: true/false.

22 What is the price of fresh broccoli?

23 What is the price of frozen broccoli?

24 When cooking buttered carrots, how would you glaze them?

25 Vichy carrots should be cooked in the same way as buttered carrots: true/false.

26 What is the price of carrots?

27 What basic sauce would you use for carrots in cream sauce?
      velouté; suprême; hollandaise; béchamel

28 To cook braised celery allow approximately: 1 hour; 2 hours; 3 hours; 4 hours

29 What is the price of twelve heads of fresh celery?

30 What is the price of twelve large tins of celery hearts?

31 The cooking liquor from braised celery is added to an equal amount of . . . or . . . in order to make the coating sauce.

32 ½kg (1lb) cabbage will yield: 1–2 portions; 3–4 portions; 5–6 portions; 7–8 portions

33   What is the price of cabbage?

34   When cooking cabbage, state two factors which affect the vitamin content.

35   Suggest a suitable filling for braised stuffed cabbage.

36   Sauerkraut is: braised cabbage;   boiled white cabbage; German spring cabbage;   pickled white cabbage

37   Suggest four different ways of serving cauliflower.

38   What is the price of a six-portion cauliflower?

39   Cauliflower polonaise is finished with:

browned breadcrumbs, sieved hard-boiled eggs and chopped parsley;   cheese sauce;   breadcrumbs and cheese;   butter, breadcrumbs and parsley

40   Suggest two suitable sauces for serving with seakale.

41   What is the price of seakale?

42   All variations for cooking and serving cauliflower may be used as/or marrow: true/false.

43   What is the price of 20kg (40lb) marrow?

44   Translate the following: courge;   courgette;   courge farcie

45   To prepare marrow Provençale you would add:

chopped onion, garlic, tomatoes and parsley
chopped onion, garlic, pimento and parsley
chopped onion, mushrooms, parsley and garlic
chopped onion, garlic, mushrooms and pimento

46   1kg (2lb) spinach will yield: 1 portion;   2 portions;   3 portions;   4 portions

47   Spinach is a vegetable that needs a minimum washing: true/false.

48 The time required to cook spinach is approximately:

   2 minutes; 5 minutes; 10 minutes; 15 minutes

49 What is the current market price of fresh spinach?

50 What is the current market price of frozen spinach?

51 Before cooking haricot beans they may be soaked overnight in
   cold water: true/false.

52 Approximately how much of the following would you add
   when cooking 1kg (2lb) haricot beans?

   carrot; onion; bacon trimmings

53 Translate the following: a. haricot verts; b. épinards;
   c. fèves; d. endive

54 To cook corn on the cob, allow approximately:

   5 minutes; 10 minutes; 15 minutes; 30 minutes

55 What is the difference between fried onions and French fried
   onions?

56 What size onions would you select for braising?

57 What is the price of onions?

58 ½kg (1lb) of fresh peas in the pod will yield
   approximately . . . portions.

59 ½kg (1lb) of frozen peas will yield approximately . . . portions.

60 Which of the following would you use in preparing peas, French
   style: lettuce and button onions; lettuce and mushrooms;
   mushrooms and button onions; mushrooms and garlic?

61 A mixture of peas and carrots is known as . . . style.

62 When preparing stuffed pimento, would you use red pimento or
   green pimento?

63   What is the difference between red and green pimentos?

64   The base of the stuffing used for stuffed pimento is:

  breadcrumbs;   sausagemeat;   mixed vegetables;   rice

65   Salsify should be cooked in a blanc: true/false.

66   What is the price of salsify?

67   a. To remove the skins from tomatoes plunge them into boiling
      water for approximately:
      1–2 seconds;   3–4 seconds;   5–6 seconds;   9–10 seconds

  b. What factor determines the length of time?

68   What ingredients are added to tomatoes to make tomato
  concassé?

69   What is the current market price of English tomatoes?

70   What is the current market price of imported tomatoes?

71   1kg (2lb) leeks prepared for braising will yield approximately:

  1 portion;   2 portions;   3 portions;   4 portions

72   When preparing pease pudding it is usual to use: frozen peas;
  tinned peas;   split green peas;   split yellow peas

73   Is it more efficient to cook pease pudding: on top of the stove;
  in the oven?

74   What ingredients in addition to peas would you add to pease
  pudding to improve the flavour?

75   Which of the following is used in a dish of mixed vegetables
  (macedoine de légumes)?

  swedes, turnips, haricot beans, peas
  swedes, turnips, mushrooms
  carrots, turnips, mushrooms
  carrots, turnips, peas, French beans

Short Questions ● Answers ....

1   true

2   true

3   hollandaise;   vinaigrette

4   20–30 minutes depending on size

5   blanc

6   Jerusalem

7   current market price

8   current market price

9   6–8 according to size

10   false, it is important to thoroughly wash them, especially the tips as they may contain sandy soil

11   15 mins, according to thickness

12   Maltaise;   Hollandaise

13   false, they are also popular served cold

14   current market price

15   current market price

16   sprue

17   aubergine

18   current market price

19   yes

20   cooked mixture of marrow, aubergine, tomato, onion and peppers

21 true

22 current market price

23 current market price

24 by evaporating the water in which they were cooked and tossing them in butter over fierce heat

25 true

26 current market price

27 béchamel

28 approx 2 hours according to age and size

29 current market price

30 current market price

31 jus lié or demi glace

32 3–4 portions

33 current market price

34 overcooking;   addition of soda

35 sausage meat

36 pickled white cabbage

37 e.g. au beurre, persillé, with cream sauce, Mornay

38 current market price

39 browned breadcrumbs, sieved hard boiled eggs, parsley

40 melted butter, hollandaise

41 current market price

42   true

43   current market price

44   marrow, baby marrow, stuffed marrow

45   onion, garlic, tomatoes, parsley

46   2 portions

47   false, it can be very gritty

48   approx 5 minutes according to size

49   current market price

50   current market price

51   true

52   4oz carrot, 4oz onion, 4oz bacon

53   a. French beans;   b. spinach;   c. broad beans;   d. chicory

54   15 mins according to freshness

55   French fried are deep fried onion rings
       fried onions are shallow fried

56   medium sized

57   current market price

58   2 portion

59   8 portions

60   lettuce and button onions

61   à la flamande or Flemish style

62   red

63   the red are fully ripe

64   rice

65   true

66   current market price

67   9–10 seconds — the riper the tomato the less time

68   chopped shallots, fat

69   current market price

70   current market price

71   4 portions

72   split yellow peas

73   in the oven

74   studded onion, carrot, bacon

75   carrots, turnips, peas, French beans

POTATOES
(Chapter 18)

Short Questions . . . .

1   State the nutritional content of potatoes.

2   Approximately how many portions can be obtained from ½kg (1lb) of old potatoes?
New potatoes?

3   Even-sized boiled potatoes will cook in approximately:

      10 minutes;   15 minutes;   20 minutes;   30 minutes

4   Parsley potatoes are cooked by: boiling;   roasting; sautéing;   frying

5   Riced potatoes are a mixture of half potatoes half rice: true/false.

6   Why are butter or margarine and warm milk added to mashed potatoes?

7   What ingredients can be added to mashed potatoes in order to make a variation?

8   What ingredients are added to dry mashed potato in order to make duchess potatoes?

9   Why are duchess potatoes dried after piping, before brushing them with egg-wash?

10 Brioche potatoes are made from: mashed potatoes;   duchess potatoes;   sauté potatoes;   baked jacket potatoes

11 Why should croquette potatoes be passed through flour, egg and crumbs before being deep fried?

12 What is added to duchess potato to make marquis potatoes?

      onion;   cheese;   tomato

13 The best way to pre-cook potatoes for pommes sauté is:

boil in jacket;   steam in jacket;   peel and boil;   peel, slice and steam

14 When preparing pommes Lyonnaise, allow two parts onion to one part potatoes: true/false.

15 Game chips should be cooked in cool fat: true/false.

16 When giving chipped potatoes their 'first fry' the temperature of the fat should be: 100°C;   120°C;   140°C;   165°C

17 After frying and before serving, chipped potatoes may be lightly seasoned with salt: true/false.

18 Which of the following are prepared from a baked jacket potato: pommes Macaire;   pommes bataille;   pommes marquise;   pommes fondantes?

19 When preparing pommes boulangère (savoury potatoes) use two parts of potato to one part of onion: true/false.

20 How long does it take to cook four portions of pommes boulangère?   20 minutes;   45 minutes;   1 hour;   1½ hours

21 Fondant potatoes are even-sized, brushed with butter or margarine and cooked in stock in the oven: true/false.

22 Which potato dish has bacon, onion, chopped parsley and white stock added during cooking: rissolées;   berrichonne;   mignonnette;   Anna?

23 Roast potatoes should be cooked in a hot oven 230°–250°: true/false.

24 Both château potatoes and fondant potatoes are cooked in stock in the oven: true/false.

25 Noisette potatoes are turned with a small kitchen knife: true/false.

26 Parisienne potatoes should be finished by rolling in a little meat glaze: true/false.

27 Diced potatoes, button onions, lardons, cooked in stock are known as: pommes au lard; Delmonico; Parmentier; bataille

28 Delmonico potatoes are cooked in white stock: true/false.

29 Boiling is the only efficient method of cooking new potatoes: true/false.

30 Parmentier potatoes should be deep fried: true/false.

31 Pommes Anna like pommes boulangère should contain a proportion of finely sliced onion: true/false.

Questions in depth . . . .

1 a. Explain why potatoes cooked in their skins retain more of their food value.

   b. What is the approximate yield from 1lb of old and 1lb new potatoes?

   c. Describe the making of duchess potato and explain how three variations can be made.

   d. Explain why fondant potatoes are so called and how they are prepared.

   e. Describe the preparation and cooking of pommes boulangère and with what dish they are frequently offered.

Short Questions ● Answers . . . .

1 approx 20% starch, small amount protein (under skin), vitamin C

2 old potato; 3 portions new; 4 portions

3 20 mins

4 boiling

5 false, all potato

6 to enrichen them

7   cheese, cream etc.   *p438 PC*

8   egg yolks and butter or margarine

9   to reduce the risk of spoiling the shape when brushing with egg wash

10   duchess potato

11   to hold the duchess mixture together, to stop fat penetration and to form a crisp golden brown surface after frying

12   tomato

13   steam in jacket

14   false

15   false, hot fat

16   165°C

17   true

18   Macaire

19   false, 4 parts potato to 1 part onion

20   1½ hours

21   true

22   berrichonne

23   true

24   false, only fondant potatoes, roast potatoes are cooked in fat

25   false, a noisette cutter is used

26   true

27 pommes au lard

28 false, they are cooked in milk

29 false, they can be steamed

30 false, they should be shallow fried

31 false, there is no onion in pommes Anna

32 rice;   pasta

Questions in depth ● Outline answers . . . .

1   a. protein;   vitamin C is under skin — most is lost when
        peeled   *p392 T of C*

    b. old 3;   new 4

    c. potatoes are mashed, addition of egg yolk and butter, piped,
        firmed, egg washed and browned   *p439/40 PC*
        e.g. croquettes — moulded, pané — deep fried

    d. even sized potatoes are brushed with melted butter then
        cooked in stock in the oven. The stock is absorbed by the
        potatoes giving them a soft, melting (fondant) quality.

    e. thin sliced potatoes, onions, stock, seasoning
        oven baked — roast lamb   *p445 PC*

PASTRY
(Chapter 19)

Short Questions . . . .

1   What pastry is used for Cornish pasties and fruit pies?

   puff;   rough puff;   flaky;   short

2   The usual proportion of fat to flour for short pastry is:

   1 part fat to 1 part flour
   1 part fat to 2 parts flour
   1 part fat to 3 parts flour
   1 part fat to 4 parts flour

3   When being mixed, short pastry should be handled firmly and well kneaded: true/false.

4   Give one possible reason for each of the following faults in short pastry: 1 hard; 2 soft-crumbly; 3 blistered; 4 soggy; 5 shrunken

5   When making puff pastry is strong flour or soft flour used.

6   The usual proportion of fat to flour for puff pastry is:

   1 part fat to 1 part flour
   1 part fat to 2 parts flour
   1 part fat to 3 parts flour
   1 part fat to 4 parts flour

7   List four ways of adding fat to flour.

8   Why is it essential to rest the paste between the various stages of making puff pastry?

9   What are the current market prices of: flour; lard; butter; margarine; cooking fat?

10 What causes the lift or lightness in puff pastry?

11 Why is an acid such as lemon juice added when making puff pastry?

12 Give one reason for each of the following faults in puff pastry:

   not flaky; fat oozes out; hard; shrunken; soggy; uneven rise

13 The usual proportion of fat to flour for rough puff pastry is:

   1 part fat to 1 part flour
   1 part fat to 2 parts flour
   3 parts fat to 4 parts flour
   3 parts fat to 5 parts flour

14 It is best to use sugar paste immediately after it has been made: true/false.

15 What are the prices of: castor sugar; granulated sugar; loaf sugar; icing sugar?

16 Which paste is used for flans and fruit tartlets? short; rough puff; sugar

17 Baking powder is used in making suet paste: true/false.

18 The usual proportion of suet to flour in suet paste is:

   1 part suet to 1 part flour
   1 part suet to 2 parts flour
   1 part suet to 3 parts flour
   1 part suet to 4 parts flour

19 Give one reason for each of the following faults in suet paste:

   heavy-soggy; tough; lumps of suet

20 What is hot water paste used for?

21 At what temperature should hot water paste be used?

   hot; cold; warm

22 The approximate number of eggs per ½ litre (1 pint) of choux paste is: 4; 8; 12; 16

23 What is the current price of eggs?

24 Name three items prepared from choux paste.

25 Give one reason for each of the following faults in choux paste:

greasy and heavy;   soft — not aerated

26 How many scones should a mixture using 200g (½lb) flour base yield?

27 What is added to a basic scone mixture to make fruit scones?

currants;   raisins;   angelica and cherries;   sultanas

28 Give four variations to basic small cake mixture.

29 Give one reason for each of the following faults in sponges:

close texture;   holey;   sunken;   white spots on surface

30 A genoese sponge contains a fat or oil: true/false.

31 The proportion of fat to flour in genoese is:

1 part fat to 1 part flour
1 part fat to 2 parts flour
1 part fat to 3 parts flour
1 part fat to 4 parts flour

32 What ingredient is added to the basic mixture for genoese in order to make chocolate genoese?

33 What should be the flavour of gâteau moka?

34 Give one reason for each of the following faults in yeast dough:

close texture;   uneven texture;   coarse texture;   wrinkled;
sour;   broken crust;   white spots on crust

35 Flour for making bread and rolls should be a strong flour and should be warmed: true/false.

36 What happens when a yeast dough is proved?

37 What two extra ingredients are added to a basic dough in order to make bun dough?

38 What is the price of yeast?

39 Give three examples of goods made from bun dough.

40 Doughnuts should be fried in: cool fat;   moderately hot fat; hot fat;   very hot fat

41 Savarin paste contains yeast: true/false.

42 What two ingredients are added to savarin paste in order to make rum babas?

43 Crème Chantilly is: plain single cream;   half whipped double cream;   whipped cream sweetened and flavoured with vanilla; a special type of pastry cream

44 What ingredients are used in preparing a syrup for soaking babas?

45 Which of the following is the odd one out and why?

    baba;   savarin;   meringue;   marignan

46 Name six fruits or combination of fruits suitable for making into a fruit pie.

47 Which ingredient is missing from the following list for the filling for a treacle tart: syrup or treacle;   lemon juice;   water;   ...?

48 Baked apple dumplings are usually made with:

    rough puff taste;   sugar paste;   short paste;   puff paste

49 What is the price of cooking apples?

50 What two ingredients are put into the centre of an apple before covering it with pastry for a baked apple dumpling?

51 Which of the following are added to Dutch apple tart?

    currants;   raisins;   sultanas;   dates

52 An apple flan should be finished with: red glaze;   yellow jelly;   icing sugar;   or apricot glaze

53 Should cherries in a cherry flan be stoned? Yes/no.

54   Fruit flans should be cooked in: cool oven;   hot oven;   moderately hot oven;   or fierce oven

55   What may be placed as a layer on the base of a rhubarb flan?

56   What is the price of rhubarb?

57   Name three types of fruit flan for which the flan case is baked blind.

58   Is the flan case 'blind' for a banana flan? Yes/no.

59   What is the price of bananas?

60   Is it usual to put a layer on the base of a banana flan? Yes/no. If so, what can be used?

61   What is the difference between a strawberry tartlet and a strawberry barquette?

62   What is the price of fresh strawberries in season?

63   What is the price of frozen strawberries?

64   What is the distinctive flavouring in the filling of bakewell tart?

65   What jam should be used in the base of a bakewell tart?
     apricot;   strawberry;   raspberry;   red plum

66   What is the main filling in a lemon meringue pie?

67   What is the price of a dozen lemons?

68   What item could be made from the following ingredients?
     100g (4oz) butter or margarine;   2 eggs;   100g (4oz) castor sugar;   1 lemon

69   What is the difference between a jam turnover and a jam puff?

70   Which paste is used for cream horns: short paste;   sugar paste;   flaky paste;   or puff paste?

71   Is a little jam placed in the bottom of a cream horn after cooking and before filling with cream? Yes/no.

72   Cream horns should be baked in: hot oven;   moderately hot oven;   cool oven;   or very hot oven

73   What is the reason for sprinkling some puff pastry goods with icing sugar and returning them to a hot oven at the last stage of cooking?

74   What is the English for mille-feuilles?

75   What is the literal translation of mille-feuilles?

76   What is the traditional filling for mille-feuilles?

77   Which of the traditional fillings for a mille-feuilles is sometimes varied because of popular taste?

78   What is the term given to the traditional decorative finish for a mille-feuilles?

79   Which of the following would be the odd one out as a filling for jalousie: mincemeat;   frangipane;   jam;   or apple?

80   Which filling is used for a gâteau Pithiviers: marzipan;   mincemeat;   cooked rice;   or frangipane?

81   To make palmiers it is essential to use good puff pastry: true/false.

82   How can you make two palmiers into a tea pastry?

83   Suggest two sauces suitable for serving with mince pies.

84   How many bouchées can be obtained from puff pastry using 200g (½lb) flour?

85   Bouchées should be cooked on greased, dampened baking sheets: true/false.

86   What is the name given to large bouchées?

87   What variation in flavour in addition to chocolate is used for éclairs?

88   What happens to the fondant glaze on éclairs if it is overheated?

89   What ingredient may be sprinkled on cream buns before they are baked?

90   How are cream buns finished before service?

91   What are profiteroles?

92   In how many sizes may profiteroles be made, and for what purpose?

93   When serving profiteroles filled with cream as a sweet, which sauce is usually offered: jam; raspberry; vanilla; or chocolate?

94   What are pieces of choux paste the size of a walnut cooked in deep fat called?

95   Suggest three fruits or combinations of fruits suitable for steamed fruit suet pudding.

96   What is the approximate cooking time for a steamed fruit pudding? 1 hour; 1½hours; 2½ hours; 3 hours

97   Give the basic quantities of ingredients for six portions steamed sponge pudding: castor sugar; eggs; baking powder; margarine; flour; milk

98   Suggest six variations for a steamed sponge pudding together with a sauce that can be offered with each.

99   Why is a soufflé pudding so called?

100 Soufflé pudding should be cooked in a bain-marie in a hot oven: true/false.

101 What is the dominant flavour of soufflé milanaise?

102 What is the top layer on queen of puddings?

breadcrumbs; baked custard; meringue; or thin sheets of puff pastry

103 What thickness are apple rings cut for apple fritters?

½cm (¼in); 1cm (½in); 1½cm (¾in); 2cm (1in)

104 In a fairly hot fat, apple fritters require approximately:

2 minutes on each side; 3 minutes on each side; 4 minutes on each side; 5 minutes on each side

105 What sauce is usually offered with apple fritters? custard; apricot; syrup; or orange

106 What fruits are suitable for serving as fritters?

107 Complete this list of quantities of ingredients for pancake batter: 100g flour (4oz); milk; pinch of salt; egg; melted butter or margarine

108 Suggest three ways of serving pancakes.

109 What is a pomme bonne femme?

110 Suggest a suitable stuffing for a baked apple.

111 List six fresh fruits suitable for fruit salad.

112 What ingredient added to milk causes it to coagulate or clot?

113 What is the name of the sweet made by the process in Question 112 and what other ingredients should be added?

114 Which spice is generally used to sprinkle on the sweet in Question 113: clove; cinnamon; nutmeg; ginger?

115 Suggest four suitable fruits for making fruit fool.

116 Suggest four suitable fruits for inclusion in a fruit trifle.

117 How much sugar is needed for meringue using four egg whites?

118 As the aim when cooking meringues is to cook them without colouring they should be cooked in the slowest oven possible: true/false.

119 Name four important points to be observed when whipping egg whites.

120 Why do egg whites increase in volume when whipped?

121 How is a meringue Chantilly served?

122 What is a vacherin?

  two meringues joined by a ball of ice cream;   two meringues joined by whipped cream;   a special mould for shaping meringue;   a round case of meringue shell

123 What is the name of the sweet with a base of sponge, a layer of ice cream and a coating of meringue, browned in the oven?

124 Translate compote des fruits.

125 What is the correct finish for a jam omelette?

126 Name four types of simple milk puddings.

127 What is a fruit condé?

128 Name four fruits suitable for preparing as a condé.

129 What glaze is used to finish a condé?

130 What is the price of rice?

131 What proportion of eggs to milk is required for a baked egg custard?

  4 size 3 eggs 1 litre (2pts) milk
  6 size 3 eggs 1 litre (2pts) milk
  8 size 3 eggs 1 litre (2pts) milk
  10 size 3 eggs 1 litre (2pts) milk

132 What fruit is used in a bread and butter pudding?

  dates;   figs;   sultanas;   apricots

133 It is not necessary to cook a bread and butter pudding in a bain-marie provided the oven is cool enough: true/false.

134 What sweet can be made from stale bread?

135 What sweet with an egg custard base is made using diced sponge and fruit?

136 What name is given to the sweet in Question 135 when served cold?

137 Add the quantities to this list of ingredients for cream caramel.

milk ½ litre (1pt); sugar; eggs; vanilla; *caramel*; sugar; water

138 Cream caramels should be cooked in a bain-marie in: a hot oven; a fierce oven; a cool oven; a moderately hot oven

139 What is bavarois?

140 Suggest six varieties of bavarois.

141 A charlotte russe is a variation of a basic bavarois recipe: true/false.

142 What is pastry cream?

whipped sweetened cream for filling pastries
a basic pastry preparation of thick custard
bavarois mixture in pastry cases
mock cream used as a substitute for fresh cream

143 Which of the following ice creams is prepared as a sorbet?

vanilla; chocolate; lemon; coffee

144 The correct ice cream used for pear Belle Hélène is: vanilla; chocolate; strawberry; coffee

145 What is a sabayon sauce?

146 Suggest a suitable hot sweet for serving accompanied by a sauce sabayon.

147 What is a zabaglione?

148 What are the two basic categories of petit fours?

149 List four examples of petit fours in each of the two categories mentioned in Question 148.

150 What type of sugar is used in making langues de chat: brown; castor; granulated; or icing?

151 What can be used to shape cornets after they are cooked?

152 What is praline?

153 How is praline made?

154 What is praline used for?

155 Name the eight stages of cooking sugar in order (from small thread to caramel).

Questions in depth . . . .

1   a. What is the difference between a strong and soft flour? Which would be the more suitable for puff pastry and short pastry and give reasons why.

   b. Give

      i. proportion of fat to flour for short pastry and sugar pastry, and

      ii. list four possible reasons for faults in short pastry.

      iii. name four examples for the use of short pastry.

   c. i. Explain the principles of making successful puff pastry, and

      ii. suggest six possible reasons for faults.

   d. State ingredients and method for making choux pastry and give four examples of its use.

2   a. i. State ingredients and method for making a Victoria sandwich, and

      ii. give five reasons for possible faults when making.

iii. How does the making of a Genoese sponge differ?

b. Give ingredients and method for making a basic bread dough.

c. What is yeast, what is its food value and what points should be observed when using? Give four examples of products made from bun dough.

3 a. Name and briefly describe four sweets that can be prepared using cooking apples.

b. Suggest six fruits suitable for fresh fruit salad and describe the method of preparation and service.

c. State ingredients and method for a fruit fool, indicate three fruits.

d. Give the procedure for stiffly whipping egg whites, the method for making meringues and briefly describe and name three sweets that can be produced using meringue.

e. Describe the following:
   i. beignets aux pommes; ii. crème chantilly;
   iii. jalousie; iv. marignans; v. palmiers; vi. ananas créole

Short Questions ● Answers . . . .

1 short

2 1 fat — 2 flour

3 false, it should be handled lightly

4 e.g. excessive 1 rolling; 2 fat; 3 water; 4 oven temperature;
   5 handling   *p457/8 PC*

5 strong

6 1 : 1

7 rubbing in, creaming, lamination, boiling

8 otherwise the pastry will shrink and when cut and baked the products will be misshapen   *p458/9 PC*

9   current market price (find this out).

10   mainly due to air trapped in during the folding process and the
     steam pushing the layers apart   *p459 PC*

11   helps to strengthen the gluten content in the flour, making it
     more pliable and better able to retain the layers of fat during
     rolling

12   e.g. 1 rolling;   2 folding;   3 flour;   4 stretching;   5 oven
     temperature;   6 fat distribution   *p459/60 PC*

13   3 : 4

14   false, it should be allowed to rest and relax in a cool place

15   current market price (find this out)

16   sugar paste

17   true

18   1 : 2

19   e.g. cooking temperature;   handling;   insufficiently
     chopped   *p461 PC*

20   raised pies

21   warm

22   8

23   current market price (find this out)

24   éclairs, cream buns, profiteroles

25   basic mixture;   insufficient beating   *p462 PC*

26   8

27   sultanas

28 e.g. cherry or coconut cakes, raspberry buns, Queen
    cakes   *p464/5 PC*

29 e.g. underbeating, adding flour, oven temperature, movement of
    moulds during baking, beating   *p467 PC*

30 true

31 1 : 2

32 cocoa or chocolate powder

33 coffee

34 e.g. proving, kneading, water, yeast, quantity of yeast, second
    stage proving, covering   *p471 PC*

35 true

36 The yeast being a form of plant life, grows on the sugar and in
    the liquid and warmth of the dough. The sugar causes
    fermentation, produces gas (carbon dioxide) and alcohol in
    small bubbles. When oven heat is applied the dough
    rises.   *p156 T of C*

37 eggs and butter

38 current market price

39 e.g. fruit buns, Bath buns, Chelsea buns   *p473 PC*

40 hot fat or oil

41 true

42 currants, rum

43 whipped and vanilla flavoured   *p473 PC*

44 sugar, water, lemon, bay leaf, cinnamon, coriander   *p473 PC*

45 meringue — does not contain yeast

46 e.g. apple, damson, balckberry and apple   *p477 PC*

47   white breadcrumbs

48   short paste

49   current market price

50   sugar, cloves

51   sultanas

52   apricot glaze

53   yes

54   hot oven

55   pastry cream

56   current market price

57   strawberry, raspberry, tinned peach, etc.   *p484 PC*

58   yes

59   current market price

60   yes, pastry cream

61   tartlet — round
     barquette — boat shaped

62   current market price

63   current market price

64   frangipane or almond cream

65   raspberry

66   lemon curd

67   current market price

68 lemon curd

69 shape   *p488 PC*

70 puff

71 yes

72 hot

73 to give them an appetising shiny appearance known as a glaze

74 cream slice

75 thousand leaves

76 apricot jam, pastry cream

77 whipped cream instead of pastry cream

78 feathering or feather icing

79 jam

80 frangipane

81 false trimmings, provided they are rested, are adequate

82 join them together with whipped cream

83 custard, brandy butter

84 12

85 true

86 vol-au-vent

87 coffee

88 goes dull

89 chopped almonds

90   sprinkle with icing sugar

91   small cream buns made from choux paste

92   pea size — consommé;   double pea size for stuffing and
     garnish;   half cream bun size for serving with chocolate sauce

93   chocolate

94   fritters   *p496 PC*

95   e.g. rhubarb, apple, rhubarb and apple   *p497 PC*

96   1½ hours

97   4oz castor sugar;   2 eggs;   ½oz baking powder;
     4oz margarine;   6oz flour;   few drops of milk   *p499 PC*

98   e.g. vanilla, custard sauce
     orange, orange sauce   *p500 PC*

99   because of its light aerated consistency

100 true

101 lemon

102 meringue

103 ¼in

104 5 minutes each side

105 apricot

106 apple, banana, pineapple

107 1 egg, ½pt milk, ½oz fat and oil   *p504 PC*

108 jam, apple, orange   *p504/5 PC*

109 baked apple

110 sultanas or raisins or chopped dates *p505 PC*

111 e.g. apples, pears, pineapple, oranges, strawberries *p506 PC*

112 rennet

113 junket;   sugar, spice

114 nutmeg

115 e.g. rhubarb, raspberry *p507 PC*

116 e.g. peaches, pears *p508 PC*

117 8oz

118 true

119 fresh eggs, no specks of yolk, clean bowl and whisk etc. *p510 PC*

120 because air is incorporated during the whipping process *p511 PC*

121 two meringues joined together and decorated with whipped cream *p511 PC*

122 a round case of meringue shell

123 baked Alaska

124 assorted stewed fruit

125 sprinkle with sugar and caramelise *p512 PC*

126 rice;   semolina;   sago;   tapioca

127 cooked fruit on a base of cooked rice coated with a glaze *p516 PC*

128 e.g. peach, pear, banana, pineapple

129 apricot glaze

130 current market price

131 6 size 3 eggs

132 sultanas

133 false, cooking in a bain-marie in a moderate oven ensures a
slow oven heat which is essential   *p515 PC*

134 bread pudding   *p517 PC*

135 Cabinet pudding   *p515 PC*

136 Diplomat pudding

137 sugar 4oz, eggs 4, vanilla 3–4 drops, *caramel* — sugar 4oz,
¼pt water   *p518 PC*

138 moderately hot oven

139 a lightly gelatine set cold sweet of milk, eggs, cream and
flavouring   *p519 PC*

140 e.g. vanilla, chocolate, strawberry   *p520 PC*

141 true   *p520 PC*

142 basic pastry preparation of thick custard   *p530 PC*

143 lemon

144 vanilla

145 a sauce made from egg yolks, sugar and white wine   *p528 PC*

146 e.g. apple charlotte

147 the Italian translation for saybayon usually made with Marsala
wine

148 dry and glazed

149 e.g. langues de chat; sablés; stuffed dates; sugar dipped
grapes   *p534 PC*

150 icing

151 cream horn moulds

152 crushed basic preparation of browned nuts and sugar *p557 PC*

153 browned nuts into caramel stage sugar, cooled, crushed

154 used for flavouring many sweets e.g. cakes, gâteaux, ice creams

155 small thread, large thread, soft ball, hard ball, small crack,
large crack, caramel   *p538 PC*

Questions in depth ● Outline answers ....

1   a. the proportion of gluten proteins (gliadin and glutenin)
low proportion in soft flour, high proportion in strong
flour   *p457 PC*
strong — tougher dough assists retention of fat when rolling
puff pastry

soft   — assists soft biscuity texture in pastry (the fat breaks
down the shorter gluten strands)

b. i. short — 2 flour: 1 fat; sugar — 5 flour:
3 fat   *p457/60 PC*

ii. e.g. excess water, fat content and mixing, incorrect
mixing, over handling   *p457 PC*

iii. e.g. pies, Cornish pasties

c. i. good basic dough, texture of dough and fat equal, rolling
and method of folding, resting, describe how lightness is
given   *p458 PC*

ii. incorrect fat texture, oven temperature, water,
flour, insufficient resting, handling   *p459/60 PC*

d. water, sugar and fat boiled, cooled, eggs thoroughly beaten
in   *p462 PC*

e.g. gnocchi, éclairs, fritters

2   a. i. Victoria sandwich — 4oz each fat, sugar, flour, baking
powder, 2 eggs.
Creaming fat and sugar, beat in eggs, fold in
flour.   *p466 PC*

    ii. e.g. beating and mixing incorrectly, quantities, incorrect oven temperature

    iii. Genoese sponge — eggs, sugar beaten over heat, flour folded in, fat is added as a liquid   *p467 PC*

  b. flour, yeast, liquid, fat
warmed flour, creamed yeast, fermenting
kneading, proving   *p471 PC*

  c. plant life;   protein, vitamin B
e.g. warm not hot temperature, minimum salt, liquid at blood heat 90°F 32°C
e.g. hot cross buns, Chelsea buns   *p437 PC*

3   a. apple pie — peeled sliced cooking apples, sweetened, flavoured, covered short pastry *p477 PC*; apple flan *p480 PC*; apple Charlotte *p502 PC*; apple fritters *p503 PC*

  b. e.g. ripe dessert apples, pears, oranges, cherries, strawberries;
fruit peeled and neatly cut, mixed in stock syrup or natural syrup with minimum of handling   *illustration p506 PC*

  c. puréed fruit, sugar, cream e.g. apple, raspberry   *p507 PC*

  d. eggs fresh, no yolk, clean bowl and whisk piping on silicone paper, very low oven temperature, cool *p510/1 PC*; e.g. meringue chantilly, vacherin aux fraises   *p511/2 PC*

  e. i. deep fried slices of apple in batter *p503 PC*; ii. boat-shaped yeast pastry *p476 PC*; iii. whipped cream *p475 PC*; iv. puff pastry biscuits *p409 PC*; v. filled puff pastry slice *p492 PC*; vi. slices of pineapple on bed of cold creamy rice *p516 PC*

SAVOURIES
(Chapter 20)

Short Questions . . . .

1 What is the difference between Angels on horseback and Devils on horseback?

2 With what are prunes stuffed in the preparation for Devils on horseback?

3 Which mushrooms are selected for mushrooms on toast?

> button;   open

4 What is the current market price for: button mushrooms; open mushrooms

5 Suggest two ways of serving curried shrimps or prawns as a savoury.

6 What are the prices of prepared shrimps and prepared prawns?

7 What are the ingredients of a croque monsieur?

> ham, cheese, toast;   bacon, cheese, toast;   ham, mushroom, toast;   bacon, mushroom, toast

8 The chief ingredient in toast Derby is: ham;   mushroom; shrimp;   prawns

9 Toast Derby is topped with: mushroom;   pickled walnut; grated cheese;   slice of tomato

10 Canapé Yarmouth consists of which fish on toast?

> smoked haddock;   bloater;   kipper;   salmon

11 What price are: smoked haddock;   kipper;   smoked salmon

12 When preparing soft roes on toast, the roes need not be floured: true/false.

13 What is the price of soft roes?

14   How would you cook soft roes: grilling;   baking;   poaching;
     frying;   or boiling?

15   What has Canapé Diane in common with Angels on horseback
     and Devils on horseback?

16   Scotch woodcock is: a game bird from Scotland;   a colloquial
     term for tripe as prepared in Glasgow;   scrambled eggs on toast
     garnished with anchovies and capers;   a game pâté first
     produced in Balmoral

17   What type of bacon is used for haddock and bacon savouries?

     back;   gammon;   streaky;   collar

18   Suggest two variations that can be made to a basic creamed
     haddock on toast.

19   The ingredients for Canapé Nina are: mushroom, walnut,
     tomato;   mushroom, walnut, stoned olive;   mushroom, bacon,
     cheese;   mushroom, ham, walnut

20   Which cheese is used for Welsh rarebit?   Stilton;   Caerphilly;
     Wensleydale;   Cheddar

21   Suggest four seasonings or flavourings that can be used when
     making Welsh rarebit.

22   A buck rarebit is a Welsh rarebit with the addition of:

     bacon;   mushroom;   ham;   poached egg

23   What is the base of a cheese soufflé mixture?

24   When making cheese soufflé, how many egg whites would you
     add to the following mixture?

     butter 25g (1oz);   milk 125ml (¼pt);   egg whites;   salt;
     flour 15g (¾oz);   egg yolks 3;   grated cheese 50g (2oz);
     cayenne

25   Approximately how long would the mixture in question 25 take
     to cook in a hot oven?

     5 minutes;   15–20 minutes;   10–12 minutes;   25–30
     minutes

26 When a soufflé is cooked, if not required immediately it should be stood in a bain-marie and kept in the top of a hot plate: true/false.

27 What two ingredients are added to puff pastry in order to make cheese straws?

28 Translate beignets de fromage.

29 Translate quiche lorraine.

30 Suggest an interesting filling for a savoury flan.

31 What pastry would be used for a savoury flan?

32 Which item would be used in angels on horseback?

Questions in depth . . . .

1 a. Name and describe three savouries using cheese.

   b. Name and describe three savouries in which items are wrapped in bacon, skewered and grilled.

   c. What are: Scotch woodcock
                 Welsh rarebit
                 Buck rarebit

Short Questions ● Answers . . . .

1 oysters; prunes   *p541/2 PC*

2 chutney

3 open

4 current market price (find this out)

5 on toast;   in a bouchée

6 current market price (find this out)

7   ham, cheese toast

8   ham

9   pickled walnut

10   smoked haddock

11   current market price (find this out)

12   false

13   current market price (find this out)

14   shallow fried or grilled

15   all three are wrapped in bacon and skewered

16   scrambled eggs on toast with anchovies and capers

17   streaky

18   grated cheese, pickled walnut

19   mushroom, tomato, pickled walnut

20   Cheddar

21   e.g. mustard, cayenne, Worcester sauce   *p548 PC*

22   poached egg

23   Béchamel

24   3

25   approx 25 minutes

26   false, it must be served immediately otherwise there is a risk of it
     sagging

27   grated cheese cayenne

28   cheese fritters

29   cheese and ham savoury flan

30   e.g. mushroom and prawn;   courgette and tomato

31   short

32   oysters

Questions in depth ● Outline answers ....

1   a. e.g. cheese fritters — choux paste with cheese, deep
              fried   *p551 PC*
              cheese soufflé — light, baked cheese mixture   *p551 PC*

    b. e.g. Canapé Diane — chicken livers   *p547 PC*
              angels on horseback — oysters   *p541 PC*
              devils on horseback — prunes   *p542 PC*

    c. scrambled egg on toast, garnished   *p547 PC*
        seasoned cheese, toast   *p548 PC*
        seasoned cheese mixture on toast with a poached
        egg   *p548 PC*

MULTIPLE CHOICE QUESTIONS

1. 'Mise en place' means: clearing up afterwards; preparing in advance; replacing items used; returning food to store

2. Which joint of beef is most suitable for salting: shin; silverside; thick flank; or sirloin?

3. To boil rice allow approximately: 5 minutes; 15 minutes; 30 minutes; 1 hour

4. Which of the following is prepared from baked jacket potatoes?

    fondant potatoes; macaire potatoes; duchess potatoes; croquette potatoes

5. A mandolin is used for: dicing; chopping; slicing; mincing

6. Espagnole is the basic sauce used for: roast gravy; tomato sauce; piquant sauce; suprême sauce

7. A tronçon is: a fillet of fish; a slice of flat fish on the bone; steak from a round fish; a cutlet of fish

8. What is jus lié: thin gravy; meat juice; thickened gravy; brown sauce?

9. An egg custard can curdle during cooking because:

    too many eggs have been used; inaccurate amount of sugar used; too great a degree of heat; inferior quality eggs used

10. In which of the following is sieved potato used?

    pommes château; pommes lyonnaise; pommes duchesse; pommes fondantes

11. Approximately how many bouchées should ½kg (1lb) puff paste yield? 12; 24; 36; 48

12. After use, an omelet pan is cleaned by:

    plunging into hot water; cleaning with steel wool; rubbing with an abrasive powder; wiping with a clean cloth

13 Apple pie is usually covered with: puff pastry; crumble; short pastry; or flaky pastry

14 The term meunière means: shallow fried; grilled; deep fried; or crumbed and fried

15 Which of the following is a basic sauce? béchamel; anchovy; suprême; or chaud-froid

16 Chicken Maryland is: boiled; fried; braised; roasted

17 Which of the following is an oily fish: herring; halibut; hake; or haddock?

18 Fish stock should simmer for: 20 minutes; 40 minutes; 60 minutes; 90 minutes

19 Beef olives should be cooked by: boiling; braising; frying; steaming

20 Junket is made from:

sweet milk and gelatine; sweet milk and cornflour; sweet milk and riceflour; sweet milk and rennet

21 To produce 4½ litres (1 gallon) of beef stock use:

400g (1lb) of bones; 2kg (4lb) of bones; 5kg (10lb) of bones; 6kg (12lb) of bones

22 Which sauce is more likely to be served with shallow fried breadcrumbed lamb cutlets: chasseur; lyonnaise; reform; or bercy?

23 Saignant is a term meaning: well done; underdone; medium rare; slowly charred

24 Choucroûte is made with: cauliflower; kale; sea-kale; or cabbage

25 A noisette is cut from which joint of lamb: shoulder; leg; loin; or neck?

26 A salamander is used for: grilling; boiling; roasting; or steaming

27   The proportion of sugar to whites of egg for meringue is:

   1 white to 50g (2oz) sugar;   1 white to 75g (3oz) sugar;
   1 white to 100g (4oz) sugar;   1 white to 125g (5oz) sugar

28   Osso buco is made with: shoulder of lamb;   shoulder of veal; knuckle of lamb;   knuckle of veal

29   A salmis is: lamb stew;   veal stew;   game stew;   beef stew

30   Condé is made using: semolina;   rice;   sago;   tapioca

31   The accompaniments to roast grouse are:

   watercress, roast gravy, game chips, chipolata, bacon
   watercress, bread sauce, breadcrumbs, chipolata, ham
   watercress, roast gravy, bread sauce, game chips, bacon
   watercress, roast gravy, bread sauce, game chips, breadcrumbs

32   Prunes are used in: devils on horseback;   Scotch woodcock; Welsh rarebit;   canapé Diane

33   A chicken cut resembling a toad is called: spatchcock; capilotade;   grenouille;   ballottine

34   A Gâteau Pithiviers in addition to puff pastry has:

   apricot jam, marzipan and icing sugar
   royal icing, almond paste and apricot jam
   apricot jam, frangipane and icing sugar
   apricot jam, royal icing and marzipan

35   Grated cheese and cream with macaire potatoes is called:

   pommes Delmonico;   pommes Byron;   pommes dauphine; pommes marquise

36   Poulet à la king contains:

   beef, demi-glace and red wine;   chicken, chicken velouté and sherry;   lamb, jus-lié and rice;   veal, mushrooms and tomato sauce

37 Gelatine is added to bavarois:

> after adding the cream; when heating the milk; when the custard is cold; when the custard is hot

38 A fish dish containing chopped parsley, chopped shallots, sliced mushrooms, mushrooms, and diced tomato is called:

> Bréval; Bercy; bonne femme; berrichonne

39 As an accompaniment to turtle soup, which of the following would be served? fleurons; croûtons; canapés; cheese straws

40 Which dish would be served as a sweet?
pomme en robe de chambre; pomme bonne-femme; pomme au four; pomme à la neige

Multiple Choice Questions ● Answers ....

1 preparing in advance

2 silverside

3 15 minutes

4 Macaire

5 slicing

6 piquant sauce

7 slice of flat fish on bone

8 thickend gravy

9 too much heat

10 duchesse

11 12

12 wiping with dry clean cloth

13   short pastry

14   shallow fried

15   béchamel

16   fried

17   herring

18   20 minutes

19   braising

20   sweet milk and rennet

21   4lbs

22   Réforme

23   underdone

24   cabbage

25   loin

26   grilling

27   1 white to 2oz sugar

28   knuckle of veal

29   game stew

30   rice

31   watercress, roast gravy, bread sauce, game chips, bacon

32   devils on horseback

33   spatchcock

34 apricot jam, frangipane, icing sugar

35 Byron

36 chicken, chicken velouté, sherry

37 when the custard is hot

38 Bréval

39 cheese straws

40 pomme bonne-femme

MIXED QUESTIONS

1   Name two typical British dishes using stewing lamb.

2   Which cuts from the carcass of lamb could be used for grilling?

3   The term for vegetables cut into thin strips is?

4   A bouquet garni usually consists of:

    onions, carrots, celery leek;   sage, onion, parsley, leek; parsley, bayleaf, thyme, celery;   celery, leek, bayleaf, rosemary

5   The approximate imperial equivalent of 1 litre is

6   The culinary term to 'sweat' means?

7   What is the name of the small item of equipment on which kebabs are pierced?

8   Name three British tea pastries.

9   Name three French tea pastries.

10   List the points to be considered when correcting a cream soup.

11   Name four herbs used in cooking.

12   It is better to overseason than underseason: true/false.

13   What is the translation of topinambours?

    Jersey potatoes;   Jerusalem artichokes;   Brussels sprouts; French artichokes

14   Melon is usually served as a . . . course.

15   List four vegetables suitable sweet for braising.

16   Suggest an interesting selection of eight suitable dishes for lunch or dinner.

17 Fried potatoes when served are covered with a lid: true/false.

18 Which of the following is the odd one out and why? Cream horns, Eccles cakes, jam tarts, cream slice.

19 Give a brief description of: a. Welsh rarebit; b. Scotch woodcock; c. Irish stew

Mixed questions ● Answers . . . .

1 Irish stew; Lancashire hotpot

2 cutlets, loin chops, chump chops

3 julienne

4 parsley, bayleaf, thyme, celery

5 1¾–2pts

6 to gently cook in fat without colouring

7 skewer

8 e.g. Chelsea buns, Bakewell tarts, Eccles cakes

9 e.g. Éclairs, Marignans, Palmiers

10 consistency, temperature, colour, seasoning, texture

11 thyme, bayleaf, parsley, sage

12 false, under-seasoning can be corrected, over-seasoning cannot

13 Jerusalem artichokes

14 first

15 onions, leeks, celery, endives

16   e.g. fresh fruit salad, fruit flan, cream caramels, Charlotte russe, chocolate gâteau, lemon meringue pie, meringue Chantilly, profiteroles and chocolate sauce

17   false, because the steam created by the heat being contained by the lid will soften the crispness of the fried potatoes

18   jam tarts — made with short pastry, the other three are all made from puff pastry

19   a.   toasted cheese on toast

   b.   scrambled eggs on toast garnished with capers, anchovies

   c.   lamb or mutton stew thickened with potato, leek, celery, onion